You Can Write a Romance!

And Get It Published!

Yvonne MacManus

PUBLISHED BY POCKET BOOKS NEW YORK

To all the writers with whom I've worked over the years—whether I ultimately accepted your manuscripts for publication or not. I hope you learned as much from me as I did from you. . . .

And with a special, conspiratorial wink at Gaye Tardy for all the laughs we shared when working together. *Pax*.

Another *Original* publication of POCKET BOOKS

POCKET BOOKS, a Simon & Schuster division of
GULF & WESTERN CORPORATION
1230 Avenue of the Americas, New York, N.Y. 10020

ISBN: 0-671-45859-0

First Pocket Books printing March, 1983

10 9 8 7 6 5 4 3 2 1

Contents

You Can Write a Romance!

Perhaps in the entire history of book publishing, there has never been such a phenomenon as the apparently limitless success of "romances." The quotation marks are used simply because the romance category book is far from anything new; it dates further back than Charlotte Brontë's *Jane Eyre*. Its popularity has—like most category fiction—risen and fallen with the reading public's moods, which are reflected by how many copies of a book are sold in any given genre.

An example of this can be found in the relatively recent popularity of gothic novels (contemporary or historical). Paperback Library (now known as Warner Books) can be pretty much credited with the successful launching of gothic novels. You remember them; you were probably an avid reader of them as well. They all had blue covers, with a young heroine in the foreground, fleeing from some unseen danger; in the background, of course, was the mansion with a single window lighted. After a few years of publishing them, all with so similar a cover that Paperback Library began to be concerned that women could no longer tell if they'd read the book or not, management decided to run a book with the same elements on the cover . . . but with green as the dominant color. The novel bombed. It was a disaster.

Paperback Library then reprinted the novel with precisely the same cover, but with blue instead of green, and sales soared. The moral? Women *can* tell a book by its cover! However, that was in the old days, before massive marketing and research—and before (hard as it may be to believe today) publishers did any television advertising, and daytime talk shows hadn't come into serious play.

At that time, I had already had eight novels published, and had worked as an editor with three publishing firms. Seeing how hugely successful gothics were, I telephoned my now-deceased friend, Peggy Roth; Peggy was then the editor-in-chief of Paperback Library. "Peggy," I said hesitantly, "what is the formula for writing a gothic?"

"Simple," she replied. "Put an innocent young woman in an isolated mansion. There is a brooding young man, and a sinister older woman. For the first thirty pages, set your scene and characters. On page thirty-one, the hero will say 'Good morning.' For the next ten pages, the heroine will wonder what he meant by that."

We've come a long way since that kind of approach to women's category fiction. It's serious business today. Though Harlequin Books was founded in 1949, few Americans had ever heard of them until the early 1960s. Back then, editors were snickering and chortling over Harlequin's romances. "They're going to lose their shirts," was a commonplace remark.

At that time, Viña Del Mar was already pretty much a forgotten author, though Frances Parkinson Keyes was still doing quite well (the Barbara Cartland of her era, though not nearly so successful in a monetary sense). Nurse-doctor novels were still somewhat popular, but losing out to gothics. That trend took over and lasted for approximately ten years. In the early 1970s, romantic-suspense began to squeeze out gothics . . . not because the gothics weren't any good, but because the public was no longer spending its money for them.

Throughout all this time, American publishers were still waiting for the ignoble demise of Harlequin Books. "It *can't* last much longer," was to be heard at many a luncheon.

Historical romances loomed on the horizon, and for the success of these, most of the credit has to go to Avon Books. Publisher of Kathleen Woodiwiss and Rosemary Rogers, Avon pumped a fortune into advertising, special displays for book retailers, and so forth.

However, what all of these categories had in common was the element of romance: Would the heroine find true love? She might be standing with her back to the cliff, accusing the villain of dastardly deeds; or never know what the hero is thinking and therefore fear she will not be noticed by him; or even a series of misunderstandings between hero and heroine could serve to maintain the suspense of the main question: Would the heroine find true love?

All during this time, Harlequin Books spent more and more money on marketing research and test marketing; something rarely, if ever, done by American publishers in the past. However, as Harlequin's profits rose and its endurance was enhanced with ever-increasing sales, American publishers finally had to concede that there was, indeed, a solid market for romances. Why should they let a Canadian-based company make all the profits? They would supply the American reader with American heroines; flesh-and-blood women who live just like the average citizen in the USA. Tentatively, they began to get into this area of publishing.

Now? Silhouette Books, Second Chance at Love, Candlelight Romances, Love & Life . . . on and on. (In another chapter, I'll discuss the leading companies, and their editorial requirements.) Romances are Big Money. For publishers—yes. More importantly (just between us—don't let on to your editor), selling romances to publishers can make the difference between your buying Essence of Aardvark or Madame

Rochas; a five-year-old VW beetle or a new Rolls-Royce (a small one, but still . . .); or spending your retirement years in a trailer camp in Pittsburgh or living the good life of utter luxury in Spain. Honest.

Romance novels total up to nearly forty percent of all paperbacks sold. Harlequin Books alone sold nearly two hundred million romances in 1981, averaging a book per second or three thousand six hundred books per hour—twenty-four hours a day, every day of the year. To quote from a recent advertisement of theirs: "In eight years, sales have increased by 800 percent, and research shows that the romance category can easily double!" Multiply their statistics times the number of U.S. paperback companies now publishing this category, and you can swiftly compute that there's a lot of money to be made by writers. Not just the well-known ones . . . but by people like *you!* As more publishers go into this field, they need more novels. Professional writers can only write so many in a year—which leaves gaps in publishers' schedules. Who's going to fill those gaps with living, throbbing romance? You are. That's the whole purpose behind this how-to book.

Writing is a craft, like cooking or carpentry. How *well* you write may elevate it to art; but first you must learn the craft of it. And like any craft, there are basic rules. If the recipe calls for oregano, and you use cinnamon, don't be surprised if your dinner guests beg off from a return engagement. Editors are, to all intents and purposes, your dinner guests. They are highly trained "chefs" who can tell good cuisine from a can of tuna with some mushroom soup dumped on it. Similarly, if the construction kit says to use common nails, and you use finishing nails, that coffee table will be firewood in the very near future.

Not only can you learn how to be a solid, professional writer . . . but you'll be amazed at how much you already know subliminally. You know because you've been reading and enjoying romances for years; you simply hadn't made the time to analyze just why some novels work, or why you're disappointed in others. It's a lot easier to write a novel if you know what the rules are; editors will be far more receptive to your work if it is done professionally (i.e., up to the expected standards within the publishing industry); and your book will have a better chance for success in the marketplace if it measures up to what the professionals turn out.

When *The New York Times* found out that I was writing this book, a reporter telephoned me and among the first questions was: "Aren't you worried about the competition? If you give away all your secrets, what's to say these new writers won't shove you out of the picture?"

My answers to this are simple. (1) If, after nearly twenty years as a professional novelist and book editor, I can't stay one jump ahead of beginners, then I deserve to step down. (2) No two people will ever bring precisely the same ingredients to a novel. And (3) I do not write *only* romances anyway. Perhaps of foremost importance, though, is that there *is* plenty of room for everyone. The need for good romances is increasing, not diminishing.

And there's also the matter of responsibility in maintaining quality within the profession, both editorially and at the writing level. Most of you already know that the romance genre is the butt of a lot of humor, from harmless teasing to disgusted derision. To those dissenters who claim romance writers are just churning out potboilers for money, I say: So was Shakespeare. He lived from the income generated by his writing. No one in his epoch could have predicted that Shakespeare's work would become the milestone against which others were measured. That his work has endured over the centuries is a tribute to his genius—yes. Still, who in the sixteenth and seventeenth centuries thought of the Bard as anything more than what today's public thinks of, say, Neil Simon or Tennessee Williams, or Rod McKuen? And if *Romeo and Juliet* isn't a romance (albeit with a tragic ending), what is? Shakespeare's writing was to entertain; pure and simple. And that's what today's romances do. They're not everyone's preferred reading nor are they intended to be. However, an intelligent heroine, in a believable situation, can be every bit as interesting as any other kind of novel.

I honestly and sincerely believe that it is in the best interests of professional writers to help amateurs as much as possible. To date, there's been a not-too-concealed condescension among professionals toward beginners. First, most professional writers received help from someone along the line of their own apprenticeships. It's only fair to do the same for others. Second, if we're ever going to make the writing of romances a serious category for fiction, the better the quality of writing, the faster romances will be accepted as worthwhile contributions . . . not just pap for the masses. There's no reason in the world why a well-written romance couldn't appeal every bit as much to ardent feminists as to less politically involved women; or men, for that matter. The basis of romances is the pursuit of a lasting, fulfilling love—who among us isn't interested in that?

However, if your heroine is *only* interested in sexual fulfillment, in "landing her man," then this is not only trite, but a disservice to the millions of teenagers who read these books. Would you advise your daughter or son that the only thing that's important is to "be married"? No. There should be common interests and goals, tenderness and respect. There is ample opportunity for any writer of romances to provide a genuine reason for the attraction—beyond the physical. All it takes is a bit of thought, and a desire to create positive, rewarding relationships as opposed to headstrong antagonisms rooted in nothing more than unexpected physical attraction.

Not just "anything" should be published simply because it falls into a particular category. Put bluntly, trees must die somewhere before books can be published. If not for yourself, if not for your editor, then for the sake of the trees . . . do your very best. You, the editors, and publishers at large have a responsibility. It is not heavier than the earth, nor as beyond your grasp as the next galaxy. Learning the techniques of good romance writing will take a little time and a little effort; but once down pat, it's like riding a bicycle—you'll never forget the rules, and they will overlap into other types of fiction as well.

You made an investment of money when you bought this book. That investment is for you to learn, to grow, to improve, and to profit. I hate old adages, not because they're repeated so frequently, but because they are infuriatingly, consistently true—generally after the mistakes have been made. But here goes: If it's worth doing at all, it's worth doing right. Your name will go on that book; if you want to take pride in its publication, give it your best shot. You've nothing to lose, and everything to gain (to coin a phrase).

Anyone can write a book; but only you can write one you'll be proud of. Most of the rules are so simple you'll find yourself laughing at not having noticed them before. However, the best news is that you're way ahead of the game without even realizing it: You can already speak, read, and write the English language. After that, the rest is a cinch!

And in case you're wondering about having a formal education— forget it. Sure, it would help. The more you know, the more you can bring to a novel. But it is *not* essential. Some of the best American writers (not to mention Abraham Lincoln) have never gone to college; some of them didn't even finish high school.

Writing, like parenting, is frequently far more instinctual than formally taught. You learn by trial and error. This book, however, intends to spare you as many common mistakes as possible to give you an edge over those who simply forge ahead, oblivious to a few easy pointers that could spell the difference between acceptance and rejection.

The Manuscript:
Your Calling Card

Contrary to popular thinking, most writers do not live in New York City. They live all over the USA; in cities, small towns, farms, and wee hamlets. Access to editors is rarely important, or even desirable. If every editor received one phone call per day from every writer he or she has worked with, there would be no time left for any editorial work to be done.

As it is, most editors perform the bulk of their editorial duties at home—without pay, on their own time. There are so many interruptions in an editor's day that sustained concentration is seldom possible. This is one reason why many editors prefer that authors write to them with their questions as opposed to telephone calls: A letter can be read when there is time or a break in the day, but a phone call is nothing more than an intrusive, disruptive occurrence and probably an unnecessary one.

So whatever thoughts you may have been entertaining about being "too far away" to attempt to write or sell a romance novel, erase them from your mind. What is important is how you introduce yourself to the prospective editor—your manuscript, and the cover letter that accompanies it, is the editor's first impression of you and your work. And as the old saw goes, you'll never get a second chance to make a good first impression. If you wouldn't dream of going on a job interview in a housecoat, with your hair up in rollers, take the time to be every bit as professional in appearance with your manuscript.

As is true with just about everything, there are rules and guidelines. These are not recommended arbitrarily, but for very solid reasons.

Appearance. Try to leave a 1½-inch margin all the way around each page of your manuscript. Be sure you double-space every single line of it (do not, for instance, single-space a long quotation). And be sure that (1) the type is clean, free from shaded-in o's or e's, and (2) that you have a good, relatively new ribbon in your machine.

When a manuscript is accepted for publication, and is being edited, there are numerous times when editors make marginal notes about the story that they intend to question the author about. Therefore, each page needs sufficient space in the margins. The reason for double spacing is so that corrections may be made: typographical errors, misspellings, improper syntax, or any number of other changes that will be required during the editing and copyediting procedures. Clean type and a good ribbon are important both to the editor *and* to the typesetter. The volume of books most editors work with is impressive. When you stop to think of the number of manuscripts they must read over the years, be sympathetic about their tired eyes! It is not rare—though hardly commonplace—for a submission to be made to an editor that is so difficult to read that it goes back to the author . . . unread.

If there are strikeovers (there, ate, etc.), typesetters will not know which is correct; if the type is dirty, and one can't tell if it's an o or an e, errors—which are time consuming to correct and therefore costly—will be made. Bear in mind that typesetters have nothing to do with editorial decisions; they receive a manuscript, and simply set what they read into type for subsequent delivery to the printer. In fact, it isn't in the least unusual for typesetters to be rather poor in English, or even to be unable **to read it at all.** Typesetters are not permitted to change a single letter or comma; they must follow the copyedited manuscript as it is given to them, errors and all. So it is to *your* advantage to submit as clean and professional a manuscript as it is in your power to provide.

However, do not allow yourself to become so overwhelmed with the possibility of error that you cannot be creative. You will make mistakes; there has never been a totally error-free manuscript, and there probably never will be. This does not, though, give any writer the license to be sloppy or inconsiderate. Now that you know why it is important to present as clean a manuscript as you can, it will soon become automatic that you'll catch yourself in a spelling or grammatical error at the moment it is committed.

Yes, pencilled-in corrections are acceptable: If they are clearly printed, and if there aren't too many of them on a page. Again, by the time you make your corrections, the editors add theirs, and then the manuscript is copyedited, what's left could be an unreadable mess. As a rule of thumb, if you have two or three pencilled corrections on a page, that is quite acceptable. However, if the corrections run for line after line, then retype the material.

Should that become necessary, very often the changes will run longer than the original material. In that event, make it easy on yourself and your editor. Say the changes occur on page 159. The "spillover" material should not be numbered page 160, but 159-A (continuing on with the alphabet as required *unless* you intend to repaginate the entire balance of the manuscript).

If you only wish to insert a sentence or two to what you've already written, turn the paper sideways in your typewriter, write them out, then pencil in where this material is to be inserted. (See example on page 69.)

All manuscripts should be numbered beginning with page 1 right on through to the very end. Magazine and newspaper writers frequently use a different numbering system such as, for instance, 4/125. This would refer to Chapter 4, page 125. However, magazines and newspapers are often typeset in individual sections; books are not. Instead, books are printed sequentially, so a straight numbering of the pages is preferred. Too, a manuscript is often broken up into chunks and sections of it handed to a variety of typesetters; it is much faster, therefore more economical, to put the pages in order if no one has to think about where this page or that one is from.

Chapters. Oddly enough, many novice writers worry about how far down the page to place the chapter heading. The truth of it is that it really doesn't matter—as long as it is easily seen. If you want your manuscript to be "pretty," then the more "air" it has, the better it will look. If you want to be absolutely certain that there can be no confusion, then start each new chapter halfway down the page.

Editors are frequently asked how long a chapter should be. A reporter poking fun at Abraham Lincoln's great height once asked him: "Mr. Lincoln, how long should a man's legs be?" "Long enough," Mr. Lincoln replied, "to reach from his hips to the ground." And this is basically true about the length of chapters: Long enough to convey the message and leave the reader anxious to turn the page to read more.

However, with category fiction, readers are accustomed to some degree of standardization. A one- or two-page chapter is entirely too cute and gimmicky. Strive for about ten pages minimum per chapter; nine, if you must, or twelve if you wish. Few people read a novel at one sitting, so it is best to give them places to break—like a commercial on television—where they can do something else momentarily before resuming the novel.

You've often read novels where there is a space between the paragraphs, yet within the same chapter. Sometimes there are asterisks or insignias inside that space. This is called a one-line break. To point this out to the typesetter, the copyeditor will write it out as: —1#—.

The object of the one-line break is twofold. You've just written a four-page scene that is setting your heroine up for a terrible disappointment. You know it, the reader knows it; but the heroine doesn't. Rather than milking the scene to fill up ten pages to make a chapter, using the one-line break will alert the reader that we are jumping ahead in time (thus eliminating the tedium of the heroine's every waking hour) to advance the story more dramatically. Or, it can be a flashback. It can be used to go directly to the scene wherein the heroine learns of her disappointment, or even to sustain the suspense for the reader by sidetracking to a subplot.

In general fiction, the one-line break is also used to prepare the reader for a switch in narrative viewpoint (usually referred to as "multiple viewpoint"). Since romances are almost always written strictly from the heroine's viewpoint, this wouldn't apply.

Dialogue.   Dialogue should be easy to read and keep clear just who is saying what. For this to work, do not run in several characters' dialogue all in one paragraph. For each exchange or reply, begin a new paragraph. It also helps to eliminate repetitive "she said," and so forth.

Here's the wrong way:

"Hello," I said, hoping it was Dick returning my call. "Miss Laird? It's me, Mona, the switchboard operator." I smiled to myself. Even though it was not Dick, at least she was being kind enough to check back with me. "Hi, Mona." "Did you get your party all right?" she asked. "No," I said, "but he should be calling any minute now."

The right way:

> "Hello," I said, hoping it was Dick returning my call.
> "Miss Laird? It's me, Mona, the switchboard operator."
> I smiled to myself. Even though it was not Dick, at least she was being kind enough to check back with me. "Hi, Mona."
> "Did you get your party all right?"
> "No," I said, "but he should be calling any minute now."

Notice that any accompanying narrative is placed *with the speaker's actions*, not separately or with a new paragraph. This also helps to keep it clear who's doing or thinking what, especially in scenes where the dialogue involves two or more people of the same sex. If there are, say, three female characters having lunch at a restaurant, it becomes very easy for the reader to lose track of which woman is saying what. This is explained in greater detail in the chapter about writing techniques.

Note, too, that only double quotation marks are used. In this country, book publishers use the single quotation mark *only* for a quote within a quote. Magazines and newspapers do not necessarily adhere to this rule, but book publishers do. In the United Kingdom, usage is reversed; they put the double quotation marks inside the single quotation marks. However, you are probably writing your romance for publication in this country (before it sells to England for British publication, of course), so stick to American rules.

Punctuation and common usage. Don't panic! Very few writers—even top-notch professional ones—are any good at punctuation. Let common sense and your ears be your guide. "My ears?" you ask. Yes. Read aloud a sentence you've written, and listen to yourself. If you pause, put a comma in the written line. If it's a whole new thought, put a period.

Dashes and ellipses (that's what three periods in a row are called) can also be useful to the novelist. Few category novels are written with parentheses; they're unexpected and therefore jarring to the eye. Instead, to set off an independent yet related thought, dashes are used. (On your typewriter, a dash is indicated by two hyphens: --.)

However, dashes can also be used in written dialogue to indicate an abrupt termination of a sentence or an interruption:

> "I'd planned to propose to her," he said, "but now I'm not so sure—"

(Or)

> "This entire situation is getting out of hand, and—"
> "Listen to me, darling! Please!"

The first example shows a sense of dangling uncertainty; the second indicates that the speaker's thought was interrupted.

Ellipses are also used in this manner in contemporary fiction. You can let a sentence hang midair, lead into a sentence with them to indicate lack of conviction or hesitancy, or use them to show that something was left unspoken.

"When Mark said that to me, I didn't feel anger so much as, well . . . shame."
"Shame! After all he's done to you?"
"I know, I know. . . ." She shrugged.

Many writers put so many periods down between words that one would think they were being paid extra for them. The rule is simple. Ellipses are three periods, followed by the correct punctuation (it's a little more complicated than that, but for purposes of preparing a manuscript, that's good enough).

"Speaking of the devil. . . ." He nodded toward the door.
"How can you ask that . . . ?"
"I wish I knew . . . ," she said.

And so on. However, don't let such things worry you excessively. The story is the main thing; correct punctuation merely simplifies an editor's working life. Do the best you can, but avoid becoming a slave to detail.

For those of you who are purists and perfectionists, you may wish to buy a copy of the *Chicago Manual of Style,* published by The University of Chicago Press. It is the most commonly used reference work in the book publishing industry—though some publishers have their own house styles. Dictionaries also vary, and again, the most commonly used one is the Merriam-Webster Dictionary. (Beware: not all dictionaries called Webster are *the* Merriam-Webster.) However, between these two works, virtually any question you may have on punctuation, usage, and so forth, will be answered. Try to get the latest editions you can afford insofar as English is a living language, still changing, and ever expanding. Ten years ago, it was recommended to hyphenate "teen-ager"; now it's one word.

How to figure out the word count.   Publishers blithely tell writers that they want manuscripts of 55,000 or 60,000 or 90,000 words and expect authors to know what that translates to in number of pages. I have met authors who have literally counted *every* single word in their manuscripts only because they didn't know how to "strike an average."

Your word count will vary depending on whether you are using a pica or an elite typewriter; your margins; and how many write-ins you have.

There are highly complex ways to estimate a word count, and some easy ways that are not quite as efficient . . . but close enough. Writers are not generally mathematical geniuses and they shouldn't be expected to whip out ye olde slide rule (or pocket calculator) to do the production editor's job. A good approximate count should suffice.

It is important to use the same type size for the entire manuscript: i.e., don't start the novel on a pica machine, switch to an elite, then back to a pica, and so on. This can *really* louse up the word count. And if you begin new chapters at one quarter down the page, then *all* chapters should begin at the same place to make your life easier when it's time to estimate the length of your novel.

Obviously, it would be simpler to wait till the book is finished—and more accurate. However, to get at least a hint of how many words will be on how many pages, let's say you've written the first chapter—ten double-spaced pages.

Ignore the chapter page and go directly to full pages. What you're going to do, starting with the top line (unless it's dialogue—ignore brief dialogue lines), is count how many words there are on it; then drop down about four lines (again, skip short dialogue) and count how many words that line has.

Let's say you average twenty-four lines per typewritten page. You'll have counted how many words there are on each of six lines. Let's say: 10, 13, 9, 12, 14, and 11. Now you're going to "strike an average." Add up those six sums, then *divide* them by six. The answer (11.3 words) is how many words per *line* you are averaging. To find out how many words per *page,* multiply 11.3 times your average of 24 lines. This gives you an average of 271.2 words per page. You can knock off the .2, if you wish; but if it goes up to a .5 or higher, then round it off as another word.

And, of course, your chapter pages will have fewer words—depending on how far down you start each chapter. But let's say nine pages times 271 words (2,439 words), *plus* the number of words on your chapter page—maybe another 136 words. That gives you a total of 2,575 words (approximately) for the opening ten pages of manuscript. From this you can pretty well estimate how many pages will be required to meet the publisher's needs.

Once you've finished the novel, count out and average as many pages as you have the patience for (at least ten at random). The more you count out, the more accurate your estimate will be. Take the total number of pages of your manuscript and multiply that by 271 words (unless your new average is altered, then use the new figure). Then *deduct* the number of words per chapter heading . . . *and* how many lines are missing at the *end* of each chapter. There's no way to predict that every chapter ending will be a full page of manuscript; sometimes it'll be half a line, or half a page. So this must be taken into consideration, too, and subtracted from the word count.

And a few final remarks with regard to the preparation of the manuscript: MAKE A COPY! A carbon copy is the least expensive, of course; but it does necessitate making all your corrections on it as well as on the original. In the interest of saving time, have your original manuscript run off on a Xerox machine or other duplicating equipment. Because of the efficiency and relative low cost of duplicates, it is often wise to keep your original at home, and submit the copy. If you decide to do this, however, be sure to explain to the editor that you are *not* submitting copies of your manuscript to anyone else.

Almost equally important—and one would think it unnecessary to say—be *sure* you have a title page for the manuscript that provides your legal name and mailing address. If you want to show a pseudonym, that's fine; however, you *must* provide your legal name as well. If you do not, and the work is copyrighted in your pseudonym, you run the risk of putting your novel directly into public domain! (Public domain is, as it implies, the status of making a work subject to publication by anyone, with no compensation to the author whatsoever—obviously, to be avoided.)

There is a way, though, to keep your true identity secret with*out* risking loss of copyright protection. You can file for a legal d/b/a (doing/business/as); the precise term for this may vary from state to state. In some states it's known as Certificate of Registration of Trade Name. The end result is the same. For a modest fee, your town clerk or local newspaper will run a notice to the effect that you plan to use a different name for business purposes. (Some states have a time limit on this, so be sure to renew if that's true in your state.)

If you pursue this route, then you can legally sign all correspondence *and* contracts under your legal business name. Do not forget, however, to include any income under this name when you file your income tax returns. Publishers are now required to send all their authors statements of earnings; it wouldn't be difficult for the IRS to track you down.

Few of you, though, will want to go to all that bother. After all, if you write a book that is accepted for publication, you'll *want* your own name on it. A typical title page will look like this (but larger):

Jane Doe
Romance Lane
Love City, World

PASSION'S BRIGHT GLEAMING

A romantic novel

by Jane Doe
(or your pseudonym or d/b/a/)

Projected length: 60,000 words (or whatever)

Agented by:
(provide name and address if this applies)

Some writers—super-cautious, and not unreasonably so—use a rubber stamp with their name and address, and stamp this on the *back* of every page. You don't have to, but it may prove a wise idea in the long run.

However, even after manuscripts have been contracted for, it is quite possible that something could happen to it: Ink spilled on several pages; a gust of wind takes chapters with it; or it simply is lost—inexplicably, of course, but lost. If you do not have a clean copy of the manuscript, you will have to type the book all over again!

Avoid using onion-skin paper for the original; and in particular, avoid submitting that copy to an editor. The type on the paper smudges easily and becomes unreadable. If it's a hot day, and the editor is perspiring, his or her hand will remove the type even as the manuscript is being worked on.

Do not supply suggested cover sell-copy, or artwork, or state that your novel has been copyrighted. Professionals will handle the first two; people trained and experienced in what will sell, and what won't. As for copyright, under the new law, a work is considered "copyrighted" at the time of its completion; a formal copyright cannot be obtained until the book has been printed and bound. So to say that your novel is copy-righted is to tip off the editor that you're a rank beginner, suspicious that the editor is unscrupulous and may steal your idea, and therefore that you may be a "problem" author. That label could end your career before you've begun. . . .

The Blank Page
Before You

If there's anything that will drive a writer to religious comfort, or a stiff drink, faster than that first blank page, I cannot imagine what it might be. There it is, glaringly white, blankly smug, defying you to come up with a good opening sentence. To the beginning novelist, that first blank page can only be compared to coming from the wrong side of the tracks and being invited to be presented to the Royal couple at the reception. It can be scary. All the things you know about yourself, the confidence you've built up in any number of areas of life, are now about to be put to the test. Will you make a social gaffe ("Hi, Princey-poo, read any good books lately? Ha ha."), use the wrong fork, spill the soup down your bodice, trip on the grass, etc., etc.? In your daily routine at home, none of these things is in the least important. They have no bearing on your world.

If you've never written a novel before, the feeling can be analogous. Happily, as a writer, you don't have to appear in person—it's the novel that counts, not who you are. The editors don't care if you have runs in your pantyhose, or if you're three feet tall, or weigh four hundred pounds. It's the manuscript that matters—what you have to say, and how well you've said it.

Most how-to books on creative writing spend a considerable amount of time on what should go into the plot of a novel. In this particular situation, however, most of you will already be fans of romances and have an excellent idea of what should be included. But if you're one of those rare people who has never read a romance (not even out of sheer curiosity), your homework will soon fill you in on all the necessary elements.

Obviously, you'll want to avoid any downbeat situations for your story; your heroine will not find herself hooked on drugs, nor will your hero be an alcoholic, and certainly no one will be a child abuser. (Though, admittedly, some of the newer lines of romance are beginning to get into more lifelike circumstances; let each publisher's set of guidelines direct you with regard to that.)

Frankly, in all my years of editorial experience, I find that novices have the least amount of difficulty with coming up with a plot. Where they bog, and sometimes fail miserably, is in the actual writing of the novel. For this reason, I am not going to spend all that much time on how to plot a book so much as on how to write it.

There are as many different approaches to writing a novel as there are people who write them. There is no One Truth or Right Way. I tend to prefer to think of a title first; that more or less sets the tone for me. Other writers wait till the book is completed, or frequently submit a novel with the disavowing "Untitled Manuscript" on it. That's okay. Editors are very good at coming up with suitable titles; in fact, they are generally much better at it than authors. I tend to be spotty about my own titles (though I can come up with dozens of excellent titles for other people's books).

For a while (a very short while!), I played around with referring to *The Oxford Dictionary of Quotations* as a source for titles. You know, something lofty sounding that I could then provide the full quote for in the front matter of the book. To show you just how stupid even an old pro can be, I was going to write a romance with suspense elements, so I figured something about "fate" might be interesting. In consulting the Oxford, I found the following:

> Ah Love! could thou and I with Fate conspire
> To grasp this sorry Scheme of Things entire,
> Would not we shatter it to bits—and then
> Re-mold it nearer to the Heart's Desire!

A little quatrain from Omar Khayyám's *Rubáiyát*. Did I choose "Heart's Desire" for the title? Of course not. Instead, I used *With Fate Conspire*. Know what everyone else remembered it to be? "With Mate Perspire." I am not joking.

As if that wasn't bad enough, I later wrote a novel (same Oxford sourcebook . . . I should throw it away!) of the same genre and gleaned: "Keep the young generations in hail, And bequeath them no tumbled house!" —George Meredith, *The Empty Purse*. So I titled the novel: *Bequeath Them No Tumbled House*. Result? Any erroneous variation you can come up with. "No Tumbled House" might have been okay, but can you imagine any denture wearer trying to ask for that book? It sold quite well; though I think it was on the basis of the illustration.

However, to this day, I still tend to want a title before facing the blank page. That way, I can write my name and address up at the top, drop down and center the title and repeat my name (or pseudonym), and then toward the bottom of the page, my projected word length. In this self-deceiving manner, I figure I've licked the blank-page syndrome. It's *not* blank; all I need now is what to do as a follow-up. A self-serving delusion, yet it seems to work.

Some writers stare out the window, others pace with glazed eyes, and some lucky few just plunge in with a what-the-heck attitude—it can always be rewritten if it isn't any good. When I first started writing, I would laboriously agonize over three, four, or more rewrites (on cheapest possible paper) before sending my work to an editor. Today, my first draft is my last. I've learned the craft, and developed a writing muscle; only if an editor requests changes—which hasn't occurred in more than ten years—do I rewrite anything.

You will not be able to do this at first. I mention it only to give you the ray of hope to proceed. The bullet will not explode from being bitten; it must collide with an object.

The simplest way to tackle a novel is to write an outline first. I am incapable of doing that. My outlines bear as much relevance to the finished product as the blueprint for the space shuttle applies to the manufacturing of lipsticks. My characters evolve in the writing; so does the story. It is a *rotten* way to write a book, far more work, leads to many excuses to run errands, and is a definite means of insuring insomnia. I could go on and on about how awful it is not to be able to write an outline; instead, let me urge you to acquire good writing habits from the onset.

With an outline, you *know* what you're going to write next; without one, every day is yet another blank page. For some people, it comes easily; how I envy them. If it doesn't happen that way for you, let me suggest that you block off some family time . . . make it a fun project with everyone's input. Even if you don't use their suggestions, more often than not, you'll get fresh ideas *because* something else was brought up.

Get a lot of ruled pads and sharpened pencils. Play "chairman of the board," if you wish, calling upon your key executives for feedback prior to launching an "advertising campaign."

Because of the variety of romances on the market today, you will do your homework first: Decide what *type* of romance you want to write (which should be based on the type of romance you most enjoy reading). Virgin heroine, no smoking or drinking; a heroine on the rebound, or a widow; a setting for her that's exotic . . . and so forth. How far should the love scenes go? That depends on which publisher you're aiming at. Before you can determine that, you should read at least five or six novels from each publisher; as you read, make a breakdown of what happens in every single chapter. For instance:

Chapter 1: Heroine loses job; meets ultimate hero by end of chapter. Instant attraction, but resents his condescension.

Chapter 2: Heroine has no luck finding a job; sees ad in paper that sounds too good to be true. Applies for job only to learn the boss is the ultimate hero. He makes a derisive remark and she's offended—can she afford to let pride prevent her from making a living?

And so on. What you're doing is "blocking out" the complete action of the novel before you sit down to write a word of your own. Your family can help; in fact, you will find them very involved, caring about the day's output, coming up with new ideas, and it can be a great deal of fun.

When you get to love scenes in a published book, pay very careful attention. How many pages are devoted to the love scene in comparison to the rest of the chapter? How many love scenes are there throughout the book? How explicit are they?

The love scenes, as you already know, are what the readers want, what they paid good money for. The extent of them will differ from publisher to publisher depending upon its marketing objectives. (Most publishers of romances have printed authors' guidelines, spelling out just what they're looking for. Send for them with a brief note, and enclose a self-addressed stamped envelope—regular business size.) Think about what *you* remember about a romance two weeks after you've read it: Do you remember the heroine's career direction? Probably not. You remember the romance. That's what these books are all about. So when you are working on your plot—having dissected what the editorial requirements are—be sure to provide at least as much romance as other books in that publisher's line have.

Naturally, all romance and no work can become dull reading. You'll need to have complications, setbacks, hopes, and so forth, to break up the story line. Some romances are very simple in story line: Girl meets boy, girl falls in love with boy, he falls in love with her, circumstances (parents or whatever) prevent them from getting together (chastely!), but all is wonderful in the end. "Love conquers all" is as good a one-line summary as any.

Some romance publishers are now seeking novels where the heroines are more mature than they have traditionally been; capable of tying their own shoelaces, able to make a living, and the only thing that's missing in their lives is True Love. Again, you'll have to research each publisher's preferences before you start to block out your own novel. Your only reliable source of reference will be to break down the plot lines of novels they have already published, weld this to their guidelines and come up with an interesting variation on the theme. Remember that these are formula books—tried and proved to be popular and successful. Do not bring in that your heroine's great-aunt was the first registered nurse in the Territory of Arizona *unless* it is essential to the story itself. And at that, play it down . . . it could interfere with the action of the novel and will certainly take space away from romantic scenes.

The general rule of thumb for any plot in commercial fiction (be it high drama, tragedy, or romance) is:

> Introduce your protagonist and give her a set of problems to overcome: job, family, health, or whatever. The bulk of the novel will deal with her efforts to overcome these problems. She will think she's going to succeed, only to fail (in a romance, preferably through someone else's intervention). She will make numerous efforts, have modest gains and some setbacks. The ending of the book is the resolution: If successful, it's a happy ending; if unsuccessful (which never happens in romances!), it's a sad ending.

Depending on which publisher you're writing for, you may require a subplot. As that implies, it is the smaller story within your overall one, and as such, should be given less attention. In fact, a good subplot should be easily lifted right *out* of the novel, and never be missed. Let's go back to the brief example already provided. Gloria Glamorous (though she doesn't *know* she's pretty!) has just lost her job. Problem #1. Is she an orphan, the sole support of her kid sister? If so, then kid sister could become Problem #2: needs open-heart surgery, is up for the Olympics team, or somesuch—how can our heroine provide for the kid? Now it's not only her own survival and well-being, but her sister's future as well.

She meets the hero, Harvey Handsome. He's deliciously sexy (virile, manly, or whatever that publisher prefers) but overbearing and pompous (he isn't really, he just makes a poor first impression). Okay.

So what? She's met him and figures she'll never meet him again. But then! Gloria Glamorous reads that ad and applies for the job . . . only to be floored by the fact that Harvey Handsome will be her boss. Maybe his fiancée is present and makes derogatory remarks about Gloria. Is she around much? Does she work there too? Just how much trouble can Wench make for Gloria? And will Harvey let her get away with it? (Be sure you read the publisher's guidelines very carefully before having Gloria's competitor for Harvey's affections set up as the designing, conniving type. As romances flood the marketplace, some publishers are complaining that this type of secondary character is being overworked. But for now, let's just proceed, and for identifying purposes, call her Wench.)

In the meantime, we still have the sister with a torn ligament two weeks before the finals, unable to pay entry fees (if such exist). So poor Gloria has to make a decision. She finds Harvey terribly attractive, but dislikes his attitude/demeanor—on the other hand, even heroines have to put bread on the table. So, against her better judgment, Gloria accepts the job . . . confident that she'll find another one in the near future, quit, and be done with Harvey and hovering Wench. Naturally, finding another job becomes impossible or too impractical.

However, what we've set up is that the heroine is making a mini-sacrifice for her sister (Gloria's a decent sort); is accepting a job she might not have taken otherwise; is in conflict/attraction with Harvey; possible hostilities with Wench; and has to worry about her sister's future. Main plot: Gloria and Harvey. Subplot: Sister's welfare. Possible added subplot: Conflict/antagonism with Wench.

We all know that Gloria and Harvey will fall in love and be happy forevermore—but *how* does it come to pass? With all those obstacles between them, the thing that keeps your reader turning pages is to find out what happens to make them realize they're meant for each other. Then, to add spice and variety, we have the subplot(s).

Of course, Harvey is really a wonderful, intelligent, passionate man. It's only because of all the misunderstandings that Gloria has failed to see his virtues (that, or he's been nursing a migraine for 60,000 words!).

I personally prefer romances where the conflicts arise from outside sources; not simply because Harvey is an arrogant male chauvinist. I find stories far more convincing, and the heroines more easily identified with, if the problems between hero and heroine are not superficial snarlings and stamping of petite feet. What if, for instance, Harvey is about to make a takeover bid for a smaller company. Gloria could meet other characters who defame Harvey, coloring her thinking about him. Then if she happens to overhear (not eavesdrop) Harvey in an argument with the competitor and he really sounds like he doesn't give a damn who gets hurt in the takeover, well, at least in that way she's going on something relatively tangible to dislike him for. Of course, none of what she's been told is true; but if Gloria, at an early-on point, tells him what she's heard . . . he'd have hurt feelings, probably think her an industrial spy, and he, too, would be "justified" in treating her unchivalrously—no matter how attracted to her, which he certainly is!

However, as you can readily see, this permits our Gloria to have an I.Q. that's higher than plant life; and because the hero has been put on the defensive, his actions are also acceptable. The reader knows they're both really wonderful people, meant for each other . . . it's up to you, the author, to keep that element of suspense going. They can have good moments together, showing tenderness and caring; or share a special experience (finding a lost puppy) and let their guards down for a while. Let's face it: They're aching to be in each other's arms . . . but you've got to keep the reader wondering how it'll all come to pass till the end of the novel. By reading the romances of others, you'll quickly see how that is accomplished: Diversions, either through subplots or by separation, or a variety of other ways.

I said earlier that I cannot plot a novel before it is written. This is not quite true. I'm lazy. I can, though, so dazzle you with complications that you'll *think* there's a plot. This is *not* the best way to go. Wrong. Do not do as I do, but as I say. Learning to block out your book beforehand can save you—and the editor—a lot of grief later on. It's a habit to be ingrained early—like brushing your teeth, or locking the doors before bedtime. The habits you develop (or fail to) right now' are the habits you'll be stuck with for the rest of your writing career. Like good posture will protect the organs of your body, good writing habits can save you from writer's block, wasted time, or wishing you'd taken up plumbing as a career.

But you should be apprised of the fact that, once you're into the novel itself, some characters will become more prominent than you'd anticipated when blocking out the novel, or that some of the situations don't work quite as well as you had expected. This is only natural and part of the creative process. You're not writing directions to your home, but inventing a story. You should not veer radically from your outline; yet, should that become necessary, then let your editor know at once (presupposing you've been given a contract on the basis of a partial manuscript). It could change his or her mind about your book, so get an okay first.

And once you know what will be contained in the story (whether chapter by chapter, or overall sequence of events), then every day's work becomes as simple as a coloring book. The ingredients are all there; you only have to fill in the blank space with the color, imagination, descriptives and pace of a darned good novel. Let the error of my ways be your guiding light to a safe harbor!

The Nitty-Gritty
of Writing a Novel

All right, you've read six Silhouette Romances and have decided that
this is really the type of romance you'd like to write. You've already sent
for the publisher's guidelines and know what type of heroine and hero
Silhouette wants. You know that they expect at least one subplot, and
that the preferred length of the novel is between 50,000 and a shade
under 60,000 words.

The guidelines from Silhouette have given you all the basic elements
they want to see in their romances. And you have now worked out your
complete plot. You have covered your bases, your foundation is secure,
and you have your blueprint at the ready. It's time to erect the building
itself. Or, more accurately, let's make a movie.

That's basically what you are doing with a novel. You are the casting
director, script consultant, cameraman/woman, director, set designer,
and last but not least, you are the "god" to the characters you will be
creating. In the movies, because it is visual, you see that the heroine is
wearing a low-cut clinging gown and she looks hatefully gorgeous in it;
the hero crosses the immense living room in the opulent Tudor house,
and pours himself a brandy. You don't need "words" because you can
see it. The heroine can smile, the hero can frown, and not a word of
dialogue is necessary to convey what each is thinking.

You must create the same "picture" in the reader's mind without
benefit of camera—just typewritten words on pieces of white paper. A
novel can be as boring as the annual report to the stockholders *even
though* it has a fascinating story. To make it come alive, to create a living
mural, is what separates novelists from textbook writers (no offense, but
they're not generally very exciting reading).

All professional writers have their tricks for breathing life into
lifeless pages. Yet seemingly idiotic things can ruin an author's intent.

You should have a comfortable typing chair with good back support,
and a table or desk that is at the right height for the keyboard. If you
can't have those things, don't use them as an excuse. I've written novels
sitting cross-legged on my bed, or arching like a willow tree from couch
to coffee table. It's hell on the back, but it certainly can be done. The
only time I've ever been totally unable to write was when I was living in
England. I didn't know *why* I was unable to write for a very long time.
But then I figured it out. I lived in a basement flat, and there was no
window where I had set up the typewriter. And if I can't stare out a
window, I'm in deep trouble. On the other hand, I've known writers who

prefer windowless rooms because there are no distractions. Suit your-self.

Another "little" item. When I was struggling to get a particular scene just right, I was bogging. I'd always turned on my radio to a classical music station before sitting down to work; it was automatic, like checking my paper supply. On this occasion, however, I wanted a lighthearted, frothy scene of ebullient optimism—and it just wasn't working. It read as if the heroine was fighting tears and putting on a brave front—not at all what I wanted! Disgusted with myself, I went to fix a cup of coffee. Only then did I realize that the radio station was broadcasting *Death and Transfiguration!* My mood was being altered, subliminally, by the music in the background. I've since switched to using the turntable of my stereo set. Knowing what kind of "mood" I'll need that day (or moods, for that matter), I preselect music to get me into the right frame of mind. However, I know writers who must work in total silence lest their concentration be shattered. You're going to have to work out what's best for you; not to the point of pampering yourself, or being just *too* precious, but discovering just how you work most efficiently.

And this leads me to probably one of the most important aspects of being a novelist. While you are writing a scene, *you must believe* every word of it! It doesn't matter if it has nothing to do with what you may have experienced in your own life—you must put yourself in your heroine's shoes and feel every emotion she does. If you don't, your readers won't. Just like an actor, you must "prepare" for your scene; especially if it's one that takes you outside your own personal experience. Novels should be an emotional experience; if they're not, they'll fail.

Don't think about precisely the right words or punctuation in emotion-charged scenes (happy or sad); get your feelings in tune with your heroine's and give it everything you've got. You can make corrections later, when you're going over the material; even if it means retyping the pages, conveying the mood is infinitely more important. You are in charge, like a master puppeteer, and you must imbue your characters with depth and sincerity.

Obviously, in romances, nothing too grim or depressing is going to happen to our heroines. However, they should be capable of sufficient depth to be able to do more than merely smile, frown, stamp a foot, or be reduced to putty because the hero said "Good morning." You have days when you awaken filled with a wonderful feeling that something marvelous is going to happen; and other days when you're dragged out, not quite yourself. So should your heroine. A salesclerk's courtesy and a smile can bring you out of a low mood; the sun breaking through the clouds on a rainy day; that old photograph of you as a kid (when your dog was taller than you were) . . . all sorts of things can change your outlook. So can the reverse of these situations: A rude salesclerk; a lovely day turned gray; or the snapshot of your mother three weeks before she died. *Use* these elements for your heroine; they are common to most of us, we understand why she's being affected . . . make the readers believe they actually know this young woman—care for her and are rooting for her to find happiness. Too often, beginning writers create static people. They are: Happy, sad, passionately aroused, or angry. They are also: Flat, uninteresting, shallow, and unbelievable.

I've written scenes where I have literally cried while at my typewriter. Five hours later, I've gone out to dinner and forgotten the entire day's work—but it's there, every emotion-charged word of it, waiting for me to come back the next day. It is unimportant that this is fiction, that the character doesn't really exist; what's important is that *you* believe she exists while you are *writing* about her. (No, I'm not talking about "possession." I'm talking about throwing yourself into the role. Later, when you reread what you've written, you then become the director and film editor; if it became too maudlin, or melodramatic—change it. You can always tone down what you've written . . . but recapturing a mood is almost impossible.)

My own way of working is to write by the scene, not by the chapter. If I complete an entire chapter in one sitting, wonderful. But I am far more concerned with credibility, with reader identification; so how many pages I write per day is not as significant to me as the quality of each scene. I also do not reread what I've written on the same day; I'm too close to it. I wait till the next day when I've a clearer perspective on it. And when deadlines permit, I'll wait for several months to reread my work; it's amazing how much objectivity some distance in time will provide.

Memorize this: Emotion is not a dirty word. Abuse of it could be.

I've read historical romances where the heroine is raped and her reaction to this is: "How dare he!" Good grief! Talk about lack of responsibility as a novelist! Don't forget that people tend to believe what they see in print—whether fiction or nonfiction. "Well, it was in the newspaper yesterday, so it has to be true." What about poor reportage, slanted editorials, and so on? And when people read novels, if the characters have no depth to them, most of the readers will think that whatever happened isn't all that bad (or all that wonderful). (As you may have gathered, I am strongly against rape as part of romance. It only glamorizes an act of violence in an era when most women are scared silly to leave their homes after dark.)

You are responsible for the illusions you create, the reactions of your characters.

Viewpoint. There is the first-person narrative (told as if the reader were hearing the story firsthand by use of *I*). There is the third-person narrative (using *she*). Then there is the multiple viewpoint, and the omniscient.

In multiple viewpoint, the author chooses two or three or four characters from whom we will learn what is happening. For this to be properly done, there must be a one-line break for every switch in narrator, or a new chapter begun. Each character can only know what he or she learns by witnessing something, or being told.

With the omniscient, the author creates a godlike situation wherein the reader is privy to what each of the main characters is thinking or feeling; and sometimes the author will interject him- or herself by tipping the reader off that there's more to the matter than any of the characters realize.

It is very seldom that either the first person or the omniscient can be handled with any real degree of effectiveness or success. It should not be attempted until you are really secure in your grasp of fiction techniques. However, some romances are written in the first person, so we may as well cover it. The wrong way:

> I stood by the window. I looked out and I thought: *Gosh, won't it ever stop raining?* Then I sighed and went back to my desk. But it was no use. I couldn't work.

Count how many times the word *I* is used. That's part of the problem with first-person narrative; authors trip over themselves with needless repetition. It ceases to become a good novel and instead could be entitled *The Big I*. The right way:

> Standing by the window, my spirits as damp as the rain that pelted the roof and trees, it seemed to me that the sun would never shine again. Sighing, I returned to my desk. But it was no use; the weather and recent events made work impossible.

Count how many times the word *I* is used. Not only has it only been used once . . . but the writing itself is far more effective, more mood provoking. If you insist on writing in the first person, remember that you must capture your reader's imagination and make her feel as if *she* is the heroine. If it's I-I-I, you're alienating the reader.

Omniscient and multiple viewpoint are rarely—if ever—used in today's romances. Again, to do so is to risk losing reader identification. Romance readers want to believe that they, too, are young and thin, intelligent, lithe and beautiful. That's half the fun of reading romances in the first place. They transport us outside ourselves, giving us a whole new image of what we're like, and a whole new world to live in and explore. There's no dirty linen in the hamper and your husband or boyfriend isn't *really* watching the fights on television, but planning where to take you out to dinner the next evening. Escape. That's where it's at. We all need to break away from our everyday routines once in a while; it's healthy. Whether you're reading science fiction, mysteries, a western, or any other invented story . . . it's escape. If you can learn something at the same time (such as the fact that gold cannot be picked up with a magnet, or that the origin of the word "panic" comes from the Greek god Pan), that's all to the better. However, it isn't the main thrust.

And for this reason, many publishers of romances prefer the third-person narrative. Without benefit of a degree in psychology, it's been my observation that women can more readily identify with a "her" than a "me." Moreover, the problem of eye-stopping repetition is avoided. The eye glances over the words *she* and *her* with far greater ease than with *I* and *me*. It is also much easier to write in the third person, and less self-conscious.

Whenever possible, I always urge beginning writers to stick to the third person until they are truly ready to try something new. Simplistically, one has to learn to walk before how to run. Which is not to imply that the use of the third-person narrative is an easy way out; some of the most complex and valuable contributions to the world of literature were written in the third person. However, it is the easiest to master quickly. Spanish and Esperanto are the easiest languages to learn; that does not mean they are devoid of nuance or eloquence.

You have numerous latitudes with the third-person narrative that you might not with other forms. For instance, when the heroine is standing before her mirror: If you say: "I looked at myself and wondered if he thought me pretty," the heroine sounds vain and self-centered. However, if you say: "She looked at herself in the mirror and wondered if he thought she was pretty," suddenly it becomes a very real, plausible question that any young woman might ask.

What you must adhere to (with all but the omniscient viewpoint) is the basic fact that your heroine (first-person or third-person narrative) can*not* know anything other than her own thoughts, what she witnesses, reads, is told, or in some indirect manner becomes aware of.

You cannot, for instance, have the entire story told from Gloria's viewpoint and suddenly switch to the men's club where Harvey is lunching with an old chum. If Gloria isn't present, or doesn't learn what happened at that luncheon by some other means (a friend tells her, the hero lets it slip, whatever), then Gloria cannot possibly know what was taking place. The only way you can know that your mother and father had dinner out last night is either because they told you, someone else saw them at the restaurant and tells you, or you went along. The same is true for first-person narratives, third-person narratives and multiple viewpoint.

It is no different from what happens in real life. You have had a best friend for fifteen years and believe you know her very well. However, you can't look at her and be absolutely certain that you *know* what she's thinking. You can surmise, guess, predict, base on her facial expression, assess by nervous habit, and so on. But you can't *know*.

If every time your lover becomes agitated, he suddenly starts playing with his left earlobe, then it is pretty safe to assume that such an action indicates his attitude. On the other hand, you could have your heroine believing she is aware of his thoughts, only to learn that his ear itched!

When someone frowns, is it from anger, worry, concern, or poor eyesight?

Now, you as the author can provide a lot of information for the reader's interpretation . . . or the heroine's. Example:

> Gloria gazed at Harvey, torn between what she knew she must do and what she wished were possible. She longed to touch him, but was afraid. "I have no choice, Harvey," she said softly. "I must leave here." For a torturously long moment, he said nothing.
>
> Then, taking her chin in his hand tenderly, Harvey smiled sadly. "I know. I wish it weren't true, but—" A frown creased his brow.

Okay. We know Gloria wants to stay, and it's quite clear that Harvey wants her to also. But let's do it in another way.

> Gloria gazed at Harvey, torn between what she knew she must do and what she wished were possible. The words she longed to say simply wouldn't come out; he had hurt her too deeply. "I'm leaving, Harvey. There's nothing you can do to stop me!"
>
> A frown creased his brow.

Now with this version, we've got quite a different situation—despite the fact that little was really changed. We now know that much as Gloria would like to bridge their rift, she can't. Hurt, maybe defensive, she blurts out her intent to Harvey far more harshly than even she intended.

By not giving Harvey any lines or mitigating gestures, neither Gloria nor the reader knows what's on his mind. The frown could mean almost anything from pained heartbreak to mere annoyance. How was this accomplished? By the words and actions chosen to convey the tone of the scene. The next line might have Gloria wondering what his thoughts are, or turning on her heel, leaving him behind, never knowing what he was thinking at that moment.

With secondary or incidental characters, it's even easier.

> The waitress sauntered leisurely to their table, chewing gum as if it were an act of protest. "Yeah? What's yours?" she drawled out, her eyes never meeting theirs.

This waitress will not get a tip. Moreover, you don't *have* to say what she's thinking: It's in her very attitude and manner. Compare the above to:

> The waitress, a pretty young woman with a freshly scrubbed look to her, rushed to the table with an aura of apology. "I'm sorry it took me so long to get here. May I take your order now?"

Being a forgiving and compassionate hero, Harvey will leave her no less than fifteen percent of the tab. The reader can instantly dislike the first waitress, but feel immediately sympathetic toward the second. All because of the way it was phrased. And your main characters, depending on their own frames of mind, will react accordingly.

If you want us to be uncertain just how nice a guy Harvey really is (maybe that merger fell through), he could be incensed by Waitress #1, or mildly annoyed with Waitress #2. If you want us to see another side of Harvey, let his reaction be a humorous one. What you direct your characters to do is all we have to go on.

Should you want Gloria to be short-tempered, you'd better provide a very valid reason for it; and ideally, she should regret taking out her problems on an innocent third party. Otherwise, Gloria will come across as a snippish, self-centered nit.

Determining characters' names and descriptions.   Most of us have favorite men's and women's names; and names which we tend to associate (no matter how illogically) with people we've known before whom we did or didn't like. It's purely happenstance, and foolish, of course. I've known four Phils in my life and disliked them all. Now, if I meet a man named Phil, I'm wary. Maybe he's a terrific fellow, but with a name that carries that stigma, I'm going to be on my guard. (Of course, if Phil Donahue invites me to be on his show . . . I'll be prepared to consider him an exception; not just because he's a talk show host, but because I watch his show and enjoy it.)

Aside from such subjective approaches, what you name your characters can convey a *sense,* or a picture, of who they are. Ronald and Stephen, for instance, have a gentler, more refined "feel" to them than Brad or Burt. That doesn't mean that Brad and Burt *aren't* refined . . . only that we're more apt to be surprised if they are. Think in terms of how names sound. Soft vowels convey softer impressions; hard vowels are abrupt, curt. If you want to hit a middle ground, a hero who can be imposing yet genteel underneath, strive for names that straddle their sounds: Derek, Alex, Robert, etc.

The same is even more important for your heroine and other female characters. Can you conceive of a woman named Erika as anything other than tall, willowy, blonde and probably headstrong? But if she's named Bibi, or Connie, the whole image changes.

Try to select names that will convey to the reader what a character's personality is like, or bearing, or attitude.

Many beginning writers pay next to no attention at all to the selection of names. I've received manuscripts where all the characters have one-syllable first and last names: Jim Smith, Jane Jones, Tom Post, etc. Have a heart and pity the poor reader; you've been living with your characters and know them very well. But they're all new names to the reader; it's like walking into a huge cocktail party where the reader doesn't know a single soul . . . not even the host and hostess.

Break up the names as best you can, and try to avoid similarity in sounds and beginning letters. If Jim is your hero, don't have Jack as a secondary character—or Jane, and Jill, respectively. The same is true for last names. Not only should you vary how many syllables there are, and be sure that the same letters don't begin each name (although if one character's last name is Swift, you could conceivably get away with another's surname being Salisbury or Santiago), but also try to avoid surnames that are too foreign to the American ear—unless your character is a foreigner, of course. While Roget and Colbert are originally French names, Americans are quite accustomed to hearing them and they are easily read and assimilated.

For the same reason of ease of reading, and sorting through which character is whom, descriptions should vary, too. If all your females are blonde and blue-eyed, not only is it going to confuse the reader, but you are also doing yourself a disservice. Let's say that for the dialogue of the preceding two lines, you've written: "she said." You want to break it up. It's a scene between two women, right? If one of them is a brunette, you can get away from yet another "she said" by substituting "the brunette replied."

If you really have to have similar appearance (mother and daughter, for instance), at least you can then use "the older woman said" or "the younger woman answered."

Moreover, how you choose to describe your characters—especially the heroine and hero—should be carefully considered. For some reason (no one really knows quite why), redheaded heroes rarely work as a suitable love object for heroines; however, the reverse works beautifully.

I tend to prefer protagonists who are human. Maybe my heroine's mouth is too wide for today's fashion, or too small; maybe she's a bit uncomfortable about her height, though the hero loves it about her (too short; or too tall for most men but not for him). Obviously, I'm not going to give my heroine acne and sweaty palms; not because there's anything *wrong* with either, but because readers who might live with either condition would prefer to think that they didn't. Whether you think it's unfortunate that our society places such great emphasis on physical attractiveness or not . . . let's keep in mind that we are writing for a specific market. Many women would agree that Telly Savalas and Jack Palance are extremely attractive and magnetic, but neither would make a good hero in today's romances. Similarly, as compelling as Lee Grant is, or as captivating as Carol Burnett, neither of them would make good heroines. (Sorry, folks.)

If at all possible, try to avoid any flattering descriptives of your heroine through her own observation. You should certainly state what color her hair and eyes are, if she has an oval or heart-shaped face, but keep it just to the facts. Let *other* characters refer to her to reveal how very attractive she is, such as how the hero is always attracted to women with tilted-up noses—in dialogue, *not* in their thoughts.

The heroine will, of course, be embarrassed, or pleased—yet never take flattery casually or as her due; though a secondary character may, if you want to make her seem vain.

Your characters.   First of all, you must keep your cast to a minimum. We don't have to meet everyone's mother, aunt, brother-in-law, and high school chum. Only use as many characters as are essential to the story. I had to edit a novel once that had—count 'em—one hundred and three characters packed into 60,000 words! It was utterly impossible to keep track of them all.

With incidental characters such as gas station attendants, supermarket checkout clerks, etc., we don't have to know their names. In fact, it's better if we don't. Or, if you wish to show that the heroine always shops at the same store and knows everyone's name—be sparing in how many you use. A *little* is a lot better than *more* in these situations.

I've a trick that works quite well for me when shaping my characters. I pattern each of them after a well-known TV or movie star, and I assign each of them a sign of the zodiac.

Because I'm familiar with an actor's gestures, speech patterns, and so forth, I have no difficulty whatsoever in being consistent. How would Larry Hagman (J.R. in "Dallas") react to the situation in this particular scene? Those steely pale blue eyes would grow hard and glinting as sapphires. *I* have a picture of him, and am thus able to convey it to the reader.

For assignment of astrological signs, I use Linda Goodman's *Sun Signs,* mostly because it's entertaining rather than ponderous. If I want a wishy-washy personality, that character is assigned Pisces. (Not all Pisces are nebulous, mind you. Don't get angry with me. But of all the signs, they are the most *likely* to be.) Pisces frequently have trouble with their feet . . . so that too can be part of the character's actions.

If I want someone to be headstrong, stubborn and taciturn one moment, and unable to refrain from lecturing the next . . . Scorpio. Heroes are ripe to be Scorpios. Moreover, it's the sexiest sign in the zodiac.

Obviously, in doing this, there's no problem in knowing how a character will react, or speak, in any given situation. He or she will respond according to how that sign in the zodiac would.

If you can picture your characters vividly, and you know what characteristics go with which sign, you can convey a sense of them far more easily.

This method may not work for you—or you might even consider it lazy—but it does for me. I don't have to spend a great deal of time creating physical appearance or delving into the characters' psyches. I already know.

Dialogue.   It was once stated that good dialogue should be able to be read aloud, without mentioning who's speaking, and still one can recognize which character is talking. Good luck.

However, spend some time listening to your friends as they speak. None of us talks in precisely the same way. Some people use a lot of big words needlessly; some talk in short, declarative sentences; some speak falteringly; others tend to use a lot of overemphasis on key words (shown on the typewriter by underscoring the word . . . which translates to italics in the book).

All of us have speech patterns and (often without realizing it) words or phrases that we use too frequently. Wow, gosh, I'll be damned, what in tarnation, you don't say, and so on. I knew a woman once who, anticipating what the rest of my sentence was going to be, silently mouthed my words as I was speaking. Very disconcerting. Yet, a habit.

It is best to keep such patterns predominantly for secondary characters lest it become tedious reading; and, of course, not overdone. If every single time you have Aunt Martha in a scene she says "Really?", it can wear very thin.

I tend to have my heroes talk in brief, clipped sentences unless it's a tender scene. My heroines, though, are usually more verbose without being chatterboxes. If I have a possible second romance entanglement (the other man), he is generally more conversational and open than the hero.

When I want the heroine to have an unexpected insight into the hero, I set it up so that it's an unusual situation (having to stay up all night to tend to a sick horse, or whathaveyou). Under different circumstances, it's logical that the hero will open up and reveal things about himself he wouldn't otherwise do. This also helps the reader to see what our heroine finds so attractive about him beyond the physical. He could be talking about some childhood incident, confessing that he'd had a devastating love affair years before, or a host of other "insightful" revelations that build our sympathy for him. All bark and no kisses can be very dull reading. (In many romances, I can't figure out what the heroine sees in the hero in the first place—I'd have told him to buzz off!)

Try to avoid written dialect or accented speech whenever possible. It's jarring and considered poor writing by just about everyone.

Let's pretend that Wench in the novel is a Spanish bombshell. She shouldn't have to say: "But dees ees terrrible, Harvey!" Wench could, though, remark: "But this is, how you say it in English, terrible!"

Sentence structure can also be used for affecting an accent. In Spanish, adjectives follow the noun. So Wench might comment: "It's a lovely house white." You can also refer to her accent occasionally, or mention her melodious speech (Spanish is very musical when spoken).

After you've established in the reader's mind that someone has this or that accent, or drawls, or whatever, you don't have to keep repeating it. The reader will remember it, fear not; and you need only occasionally make reference to it thereafter.

As mentioned earlier, it's important—for the sake of clarity—to keep the action of the speaker with the dialogue. Wrong way:

> Gloria listened to Wench with disbelief. She moved toward her, dark eyes flashing.
> "I'm warning you . . . he's mine!"
> "Don't you think that it's up to him?"
> She smiled sardonically.
> "He isn't aware of it, but he does what I say."

Who's saying or doing what? Right way:

> Gloria listened to Wench with disbelief.
> "I'm warning you . . . he's mine!" Wench moved toward her, dark eyes flashing.
> "Don't you think that it's up to him?"
> She smiled sardonically. "He isn't aware of it, but he does what I say."

See how much simpler it is to keep track of speaker and action? And if we already know Wench has dark eyes, her name wouldn't be needed at all.

A sampling of frequent problems in writing. The list is far longer than what is included here, but these are some of the ones to watch for.

Chapter titles: Almost never used in contemporary fiction. Don't bother.

The use of "for": Harvey stopped in his tracks for he had seen the problem immediately. Nowadays, it is less dated and smoother reading to use a semicolon instead of the word "for": Harvey stopped in his tracks; he had seen the problem immediately.

Try to avoid standard clichés about women. We don't all put our hands to our throats or mouths when surprised or frightened; I've never met a woman who stamped her foot in anger; and we don't all burst into tears if things aren't going our way.

And whether in first- or third-person narrative, don't cop out with phrases such as "but more about that later." That is to impose yourself upon the reader; worse, how can your heroine possibly know what might happen in the future?

When writing about your heroine's thoughts, do not put them in quotation marks. Quotation marks are for dialogue, or to set a word apart from the rest of the text. A general guide is that thoughts are left in roman type (i.e., the same kind of typeface you're reading right now). However, if it is the heroine's exact thinking process, then this is set off in italics.

> Gloria moved toward the railing of the ship, wondering where Harvey might be at that moment.

> Gloria moved toward the railing of the ship. *I wonder where Harvey is right now,* she thought.

Another common mistake is characters who "sit in chairs" or dogs "jumping in laps." You sit *on* a chair, not *in* it. To be *in* it, the upholstery would have to come undone and you would be "inside" the chair instead of *on* it. The same is true for animals jumping on furniture or people.

And here are just a few of the most commonly misused words:

Affect/effect: "Affect" is a verb; "effect" is a noun. You are *affected* by the loss of a lover, a cut in salary, or the weather. However, the *effect* of any of these events can be profound. Be careful about *effect,* though, because it can be tricky. It can also be used as a verb, in the sense of "bringing about": He strove to *effect* a change in the bylaws.

Blond/blonde: Technically, since the word comes from the French, "blond" is masculine, and "blonde" is feminine. Many publishers are just dropping the *e* altogether; however, you should know the difference.

Continual/continuous: *Continual* is like blowing your nose when you have a cold; you do it lots, but not constantly. *Continuous,* however, is without interruption—like a *continuous* line.

Everyone/they: As commonly used as a toothbrush; still, few people use it correctly. You cannot say: "If everyone knew the facts, they would believe her innocent." Why? Think about it for a second. "Every*one*" is singular; therefore, to use "they" with it is incorrect. Instead, say: "If all of them knew the facts," etc.; then it's correct.

Flout/flaunt: This one really gets four stars for misuse. To *flout* is to be scornful or to mock; to *flaunt* is to indulge in conspicuous display. You can *flout* someone's political opinions, or people can *flout* the rules. However, when you drive home in that new Rolls-Royce and deliberately leave it in the driveway so the neighbors can see—you're *flaunting*.

From/than: Though you'll hear it all the time, it is not proper to say "different than." An object or person is "different *from,*" not "than."

Further/farther: *Further* is used today more in the abstract than in Olden Times. One discusses a problem *further. Farther* is now used almost exclusively to indicate distance; for example, "Don't take another step farther."

Hung/hang: The laundry has been *hung* (and we all know what it means in slang usage, don't we?); however, a person is *hanged,* not hung (unless you mean it in the slang sense—better suited to males than females).

Lie/lay: Ahh yes . . . everyone's nemesis (even some editors have yet to get the hang of it). And for sure, the problem is shiftier than most espionage novels. However, if you keep it clear in your head just what each word means, you'll find it simpler to deal with . . . and which tense to use. To *lie* is to recline; to *lay* is to put down, or set something. Contrary to the convenient guideline that it has anything to do with animate or inanimate objects, it is the meaning of each that determines which is correct. If you picked up a small statue and decided to put it on its side, you are going to *lay* it on its side. If you are referring to the statue's position, it is *lying* on its side. If, though, you are moving a magazine from the coffee table, it cannot possibly stand on its own— you will *lay* it elsewhere. A chicken *lays* an egg because it is "placing" the egg somewhere. But when a kitty curls up for a nap, it is *lying*.

Proved/proven: I'm probably so outnumbered with people using these two interchangeably that, for all I know, maybe it's okay as a result of majority common usage. However, as you know, the tense structure for this is: prove, proved, proven. *Prove* is present tense; *proved* is preterite; and *proven* is the past participle. Therefore, one should say "It was *proved*" or "It has been *proven.*"

That/which: This has to do with restrictive and nonrestrictive, and all that complicated stuff. To borrow from editor-friend Shirley Peterson, think of it this way: "The cow, which has four legs, ran across the meadow"; however, "the cow that has three legs tried to run across the meadow." The first example is "nonrestrictive"; cows usually have four legs. Notice, too, that when *which* is used, it is like an aside, and is set off with commas. *That,* however, is "restrictive" insofar as it sets a three-legged cow apart from the others.

That/who: Another pet peeve of mine—the word *who* is practically disappearing from our language unless used in a question. Nonhuman things or corporations, etc., are *that;* people are *who.* So when Judy Garland sang "The Man That Got Away," the lyricist slipped her a grammatical error. It was the man *who* got away. Maybe he was an English teacher!

If you need considerably more help than just these few examples, I urge you to go to the library and borrow *Thirty Days to Better English,* and *Better English,* both by Norman Lewis. (With any luck at all, perhaps some smart publisher will republish these two books.) Also vitally important is Strunk and White's *Elements Of Style*—a gem of a book that, in a nutshell, emphasizes that simple is best; do not use a big word if a smaller one will do just as well. This book is currently available in paperback.

Descriptives in narrative. There are times when dwelling on descriptions of locale, weather, house, etc., can be very useful to establish the tone of a scene, or to be sure the reader is fully apprised so that some development later on doesn't come as an unfair surprise. The latter is generally referred to as "planting clues." And no, this isn't only used in mysteries; it's perfectly valid in general fiction and romances, too.

However, too frequently, novices will dwell endlessly and it totally stops the flow of the story. We don't really have to know that her blue dress was made of cotton, had a sweet yoke, with little buttons at the sleeves, and a Peter Pan collar, with a pleated skirt, and a matching belt, or whether her handbag and shoes were dyed to match. Give your reader a little credit for a good imagination. If a full description is vital, okay; otherwise a hint will suffice. And this is really another area where you, as "god," can give the reader a minimum amount of information that *also* reveals a great deal in a limited number of words . . . and without stopping the flow of the story.

If your hero lights his cigarettes with a book of matches, we get one picture; if he uses an eighteen-karat Cartier lighter, we get quite another. When the heroine jumps into her car, is it a beat-up old Toyota, or a nearly new Chrysler LeBaron? We don't have to know what color the car is unless it was custom-painted to match her eyes—which no romance heroine would dream of doing, but rich secondary characters might.

Should Harvey's lighter be monogrammed, this can be mentioned the first time he lights a cigarette . . . but then forget it—unless it's a clue.

Here's a typical beginner's way of describing something:

> Harvey reached in his pocket for a cigarette. He pulled out
> a lighter. It was a lovely, rich-looking one. Gloria was sure it
> was real gold. She looked at him. Harvey was so wonderfully
> handsome in his dark blue, serge, double-breasted suit. It set
> off his dark blue eyes, and the flame from his lighter made
> the color all the more intense.
> The restaurant they were at was charming. Checkered
> tablecloths were on every table along with a fresh-cut flower.
> A candle flickered between Gloria and Harvey, and it seemed
> very romantic. The restaurant was crowded, but Gloria didn't
> care. She was with Harvey and that was all that mattered.
> Soon the waiter came to take their order.

Now, my parents, relatives, and friends might think that's a terrific
description. Really sets the scene and mood. But does it? Let's try it
again.

> Seated at the round, corner table of the charming French
> restaurant, Gloria was delighted with the checkered table-
> cloths, flickering candles and fresh-cut flowers on every
> table.
> "I hadn't expected it to be so crowded tonight," Harvey
> apologized, lighting a cigarette with his gold Cartier.
> Glancing at him momentarily, Gloria couldn't help noticing
> how handsome he looked in his dark serge suit. Her mind
> briefly wandered with romantic fantasies until the waiter
> came to take their order and her little game was interrupted.

See the difference? In the first version, it is the author who is telling us
what everything is like. In the second, it is a part of what the heroine is
seeing and thinking—a much smoother way to present the same information, without interruption of its flow.

The more you can keep yourself, as author, out of the novel, the
better. Give the observations through your heroine's eyes. And with that
in mind, take stock that what your heroine (through you) elects to notice
can be highly revealing about her as a person. If all she ever notes is that
cuffs are frayed, furniture needs to be reupholstered, buttons are missing, someone's teeth should have been capped . . . well, clearly, she is a
rather negative person. That's not to say that she can't or shouldn't
notice negative things, only that there should be a balance—heavily
weighted in favor of positive observations.

Lesser characters—particularly villains—may be complainers,
whiners, and only seeing the "bad" in the world. If our heroine sees such

things, they should be accompanied with sympathy, empathy, or compassion.

How things are presented is every bit as important. If Harvey is meeting Gloria for a cocktail (she'll have a glass of white wine, thank you), and the moment she enters the room he tells her she has a run in her stocking or her slip is showing—well, that's not very sensitive to her feelings nor is it chivalrous. A "gentleman" would not mention it at all, or wait till a discreet moment to point it out.

To sidetrack for just a moment, if you don't already have a recent, good book on contemporary etiquette, I plead with you to get one—even secondhand. So many, many writers put their heroines into wealthy surroundings, and the authors haven't the foggiest notion about how a table is properly set, correct seating of guests, cutlery for specific courses of the meal, which wines to serve with what, and so forth. I read a romance a few years ago where the heroine began to eat before her hostess had lifted her fork, and a chilled Burgundy was served with fruit salad! First of all, no guest should begin to eat until his or her hostess does; Burgundy is never chilled; and to serve Burgundy with a fruit salad is like having a martini with an ice cream cone.

Again, it is your responsibility as author to make your novels as believable as possible—a minimum of checking up on etiquette can spare you a lot of embarrassment. (And no, don't count on your editor being up on such things. It is *your* job, not your editor's, to find out what's proper. Your editor's only responsibility is to be sure that the company is publishing a good, readable yarn, free from spelling and grammatical errors—accuracy is up to you.)

Getting back to descriptives in narrative. In order to present the information in such a way that the reader is hardly even aware of it, do not stop your story to describe something. The best way is to slide it in unobtrusively; the reader will create the rest. Wrong:

> Harvey crossed the room. He sat down on the red chair and unfolded the newspaper he was carrying. His eye fell on the note that was on the table next to the chair. It was addressed to him. He picked it up and opened it.

With this example, all we know about the scene is that there's a red chair. We get no picture of it at all; he could be at the doctor's office, an airport waiting lounge, or his own living room. Here's another way:

> Crossing the room, Harvey sank onto the red wingback chair and unfolded his copy of *Romantic Times*. For a moment, he let his mind wander, thinking about the beautiful job of redecorating Gloria had done for him. Gone now were the clumsy, heavy pieces of Victorian furniture. In their

place, Gloria had selected an eclectic combination of antiques—mostly English. The room now suited Harvey. It reflected his personality wonderfully, from the stately mahogany secretary to the inlaid end table beside him.

Then, as he glanced about appreciatively, his dark blue eyes fell on the small white envelope propped up between the Chinese lamp and Tiffany ashtray on the end table. His name was neatly written on it, and Harvey picked the envelope up, wondering what it contained as he opened it.

Again, it is not the author telling us what the room looks like, but the character. However, this could easily be done in segments as opposed to one section. Each time someone is in that room, a little bit can be described with the action of the story. Gloria standing beside the English antique secretary (it's then unimportant if it's mahogany or not); Harvey going to the window and pulling away the floral print curtains; and so on. It can also be done within what is used with dialogue:

Twisting the brown leather strap of her handbag, Gloria said: "Now see here!"
He turned from her, brushing at his gray flannel slacks. "What can I say?"
She exhaled heavily and perched on the edge of his Mediterranean desk. "Why do we always have to argue?"

By choosing what people surround themselves with, you can tell the reader a great deal about the character's personality. If the desk is cluttered, we know that Harvey is unorganized; if he's wearing jeans, he's far more casual than if he's wearing gray flannel slacks. This saves you from having to tell the reader about such things; they're implied by the "props" you provide.

Pace and rhythm. Rhythm? But this is prose, not poetry! Right. However, prose, too, has to have pace and rhythm. Probably the most consistent error made by beginning writers is not recognizing this. Flip back and take a look at all the examples I've provided thus far. You will notice one thing in particular: Each of the "wrong" versions is slow reading, dull and lifeless. Each of the "right" ones has pace and rhythm, is easy reading, and more fun. Why are the former examples dull? Because they are written totally in the preterite. "He walked over." "She sat down." "They held hands."

Don't forget your novel is a moving mural on paper!

Break up the tenses. Instead of saying that Gloria "decided to go to the movies, then changed her mind" (all past tense), say: "Gloria thought about going to a movie, then decided against it." In thinking about "going" you are projecting a future action; not just what didn't happen, all in the past. "She wondered if she should telephone Harvey." Future action implied by what she might do, not what she's done.

And there is the uppermost important use of the present participle. A present participle is simply the tense of the verb that ends with *ing*. Going, moving, sitting and so forth. It is not to be overworked or it can be equally boring. But when used carefully, it can really break up the rhythm of your novel.

Instead of "she sat down," think in terms of "sitting down, she—" or instead of "she gazed out the window," try "gazing out the window, she—" It gives the writing a feeling of immediacy, as if we're right there with the heroine.

By inserting the future and the present participle where each is appropriate, you take your novel out of the static past tense and give it life. Again: Do *not* overuse either.

Think about picture and action verbs, too. If Gloria sits down, that tells us next to nothing. However, if she perches, that's quite different. Verbs can also reveal the characters' moods, sometimes even more effectively than long explanations. Does Gloria walk across the room, or does she stride, amble, or saunter? If she's tired, let her sink onto the divan instead of just sitting. Teenage character who's just had a fight with Gloria? He or she would slump, hands stuffed into pockets—yes, you can slump onto a chair . . . ask any parent of a teenager.

Slamming a door makes quite a different impression from merely closing it. Create images for your readers that give your novel a sense of visual reality. Let your characters stretch to reach something, twist in their chairs, wallow in luxurious mink and so forth.

Remind yourself constantly that a novel is not a term paper. It must capture the reader's imagination with vivid actions that reveal attitudes.

Another way is to introduce sentences with prepositional phrases: "In that case, Gloria thought, she might as well have stayed home." Or: "Up till then, she'd had no choice."

Yes, the predominant part of your novel will be in the past tense— but break it up! You'll want long sentences, short ones; past tense, future indicative; gerunds, opening with prepositional phrases . . . and let's not forget punctuation. It, too, can create an illusion.

Another area where the novice tends to lose the reader is in prolonged dialogue. It's as if writers think that nothing else could be happening just because someone is speaking. How often have you been on the telephone and made notes to yourself, or taken something out of the refrigerator, or interrupted yourself to tell someone something? Have you never been in the process of leaving a room, then called out a reply to the person you've left behind? Doesn't your mind ever wander while someone is talking?

Just because a person is talking doesn't mean that person has ceased to exist other than as a disembodied voice. Some of us doodle while on the telephone, remember being low on facial tissues, or have our memories jogged about something that happened long ago.

> "How about a steak and mashed potatoes?" Harvey asked her, spreading the menu out before him.
> "The steak sounds fine, but I'll have sliced tomatoes instead," she replied, recalling all too well how long it had taken her to drop those extra five pounds.

Harvey's doing something while talking, and Gloria is remembering something. Then, if it's just the two of them in that scene, you can occasionally drop to dialogue only:

> "Worried about your weight?"
> She nodded.
> "You shouldn't be, you look great."

No problem at all keeping track of who's saying what . . . and it breaks up the pace of the book.

So do contractions. Many writers think it's permissible to use contractions in dialogue, but forget to use them in narrative. To provide enough rhythm to hold your reader's interest, there's nothing wrong with using contractions in the narrative. (My sainted English teacher will kill me, but this is fiction, not a book report!)

> She'd have to move quickly.
> He'd never listened to her.
> She hadn't thought of that before.
> Why couldn't he see reason?

Then, too, there's the matter of "eye-stopping" words. Most of us read and assimilate information almost at a glance, not even particularly aware of the individual words. However, some words stick in our minds and we remember them if they are repeated too quickly—giving the book a reputation for repetitiousness.

If you've used, say, "fascinating" in paragraph one, don't use it again in paragraph five. It's too soon. Wait at least another eight or nine pages before using it again. And the same is true of any word that is not ordinary to our mental "ears." Unusual colors, for instance, will stick in the reader's mind. If somebody "hisses" a line, don't use "hiss" again for at least another chapter.

And there are two words that have driven me crazy for years. Usually, words have synonyms to substitute with; "nightmare" has none, and the synonyms given for "smile" aren't synonyms at all. A smile is not a grimace, nor a smirk, nor a laugh, etc. So if you don't want your character to sound as if she's had a frontal lobotomy, be *very* careful with how often you use "smile."

Cliff-hangers. This is just what it sounds like and applies to the end of each chapter. To varying degrees, every chapter should end with a "cliff-hanger"; that is, a device that makes the reader want to quickly get to the next chapter. It can be a question, a statement, an unexpected development in the story, and any number of other things.

You've written that Harvey and Gloria have had an argument, and you're at the end of a chapter halfway through the book. You could end that chapter with: "Gloria sobbed her heart out." That's sort of final and doesn't pique the reader's curiosity. But if you wrote: "Gloria sobbed her heart out. Would she ever see Harvey again?" Ah, now our reader thinks: Say, how *will* those two get together after what's happened?

How about a really dreadful stormy night and you've reached the end of that chapter. Instead of saying "Gloria curled up with a good book," why not say "Gloria curled up with a good book, lost in her reading. Suddenly, she thought she heard a knock at her door. *That's funny,* she thought. *Who'd be out on a night like this?"* Well, now the reader is equally curious; who *is* at her door on such a night?

I cannot tell you how many romances have remained on my coffee table, opened to the second or third chapter, and I never finished reading them. I lost interest. I didn't care what happened next simply because the author failed to make me want to know.

Details. One of the reasons I'm so very fond of editorial work is that it permits me to be an armchair detective. You're halfway through a manuscript and the writer mentions the red-haired niece. Wait a minute! Didn't the author state that the niece was bald a few chapters back? Flip-flip-flip. Right. Gotcha.

I was reading a romance not too many years ago wherein the heroine was a guest in someone's home. Shown to her bedroom, she was pleased with how sunny it was, but the adjoining bathroom had no shower; only a claw-legged old-fashioned tub. Guess what? The heroine took six showers in that same bathroom before the book was finished. (Now *that* should have been caught by the editor . . . but wasn't. You can't trust anybody these days!)

My own way of solving this little problem is quite inexpensive, simple, and I don't have to clutter my mind trying to remember every single thing I've said on paper. I have a looseleaf notebook. For every single character (unless it's one who's a one-shot and will never appear in the book again—like a train conductor or an usher), I keep a log of everything I've ascribed to that person: physical appearance, gestures, pet expressions, where that character lives (I even make a crude drawing of the floor plan so I don't have her turning left into the kitchen in one scene, and turning right in another), background (family and personal), education—everything!

This saves me hours and hours of having to double-check myself. It also means that if the editor who is assigned to my novel happens to have a hangover, I don't have to worry about his or her not catching my mistakes. As the novel is being written, when I'm rereading yesterday's material for content and mistakes, I write down what I've said about decor, locale, and the characters themselves.

And I hold onto that looseleaf notebook until the book is not only contracted for, but published. It's generally about a year between contract and publication . . . plus the amount of time the book was being submitted to the editor(s). Who could possibly remember a question about some small detail all that while later? Much less where the information might appear in the manuscript. . . . I had a novel published last year that was completed and sent to the editor in August of the year before—almost a year had passed before the book was scheduled for publication. When it came time for the editor to go to the art meeting with regard to the cover, she telephoned me with a hasty request for a refresher on what two of the characters looked like. No problem. Out came the notebook, and I was able to tell her anything she wanted to know.

You'll sleep easier if you have all that information about your characters neatly and handily in one place.

Writer's block.   I believe it exists because I am so frequently told that it has happened to writers. However, it has never happened to me, nor to the majority of professional writers I've known over the years. Writer's block should not be lumped in with emotional trauma or illness; if you've just lost your wedding ring, or your husband is sick in bed, or you're coming down with a cold . . . that's not writer's block. That's a very good reason for not being able to think about the novel you're working on; other pressures prevail.

Now, I don't want to seem like a hard-nosed taskmaster, but I genuinely believe that—more often than not—anyone suffering from writer's block is simply self-serving and too precious for words. If you've blocked out your romance, know what it must contain, there's not a reason in the world why you can't write it. A raging case of spring fever does not equate with writer's block. Writers write; amateurs or self-pampering pros find excuses.

Still, putting aside my own prejudicial thinking about this, let's assume you have a bona fide case of writer's block. My only advice to you is keep on writing, no matter what. Even if you have to throw that day's or week's output down the drain, keep on writing. If you give in to yourself, it could become a permanent case of mental paralysis. You'll come out of it, and probably with even better ideas than before it happened.

And should it happen that you fail to take my advice about plotting out your romance before you write a line . . . even that's not a good excuse for writer's block. Because I am not a "morning person," I spend the first few hours of coming to grips with the day by doing menial tasks: run the vacuum cleaner, wash up those crystal goblets that look as if they'd spent the winter in the barbecue pit, or whatever. Since I also don't have an outline to refer to when it's time for me to sit down to work, I let my mind wander over yesterday's scenes or chapters, review what went on before then, and idly wonder what might be fun to have happen next.

Unfortunately, I, too, often box myself into a corner with this lack of discipline. Writing *With Fate Conspire,* I was typing along productively and found myself at the end of a chapter (more or less) and had to figure out what to do next for a cliff-hanging scene. I don't know why (temporary insanity, probably), but I decided that the mistress of the house should be stabbed. So I stabbed her. There she was, poor old thing, standing in the doorway with a knife handle protruding from her abdomen, telling the heroine to flee.

Now what? I hadn't planned for that to happen at all!

I telephoned a friend and we chatted aimlessly. "I just stabbed *Señora* de Lorca," I said.

"You what? But why?"

"I don't know. It seemed reasonable at the time."

"But what are you going to do next?"

I mumbled something about not having the foggiest idea. We hung up, I made a cup of coffee, then stared at the pages I'd just written. *Okay, smartie .. . is the* señora *going to die?* I had no reply for that. Shrugging, I decided that the *señora*'s fate could be determined later. I'd set it up that the heroine had to flee—and flee she did. Okay. Once back into the story, it again began to write itself. I could've knocked off for the day with the excuse of "writer's block," but it wouldn't have been true. The truth, clearly, was that I had not written an outline first and had thus made my life more difficult.

Another thing you'll hear from any number of writers—surely none of you, however!—is that they can't write a line without a drink beside them. A real drink—booze. To this I say: Cowpuckie. If you don't need a drink to write a letter, you don't need one to write a novel. Mind you, I enjoy my evening cocktail as much as anyone else; but alcohol does not make me a better writer. In fact, quite the reverse. Absolutely stupid ideas take on the veneer of Tolstoyian brilliance—when rereading in the cold light of sobriety, I have to admit I simply wasted my time. Worse, with a couple of drinks in me, my manuscript reads as if it had been typed on a Russian typewriter; my fingers get caught between the keys somehow, and what I should have done was take either a cold shower or a nap. So if I know I have a luncheon engagement with someone, and that there's likely to be more than one Bloody Mary consumed, I already know that it will be futile to attempt to work that afternoon. Better that I should spend that time telephoning all the friends I've neglected because I've been on deadline.

If you don't want to write that day, don't blame it on writer's block or because you might need a drink to rev up your creative juices. Just admit you don't feel like writing.

We will now have a brief musical interlude. . . .

The Worst Is Over . . . Or Is It?

To people who have never written a novel, it would appear that the hardest part of all is the writing. That's not necessarily true. Writing a book is a gamble, no different from putting your money on Red 16 in roulette. You have to have a strong stomach, a healthy heart, nerves of steel, and an Olympian sense of humor. Your attitude and professionalism—which I hope this book accomplishes—can make the next stage bearable. Otherwise, it can be sheer agony.

Your romance novel is completed, typed neatly and ready to send off. Send off *where?* Directly to the publisher? Or maybe you should find a literary agent? You don't know a thing about the book publishing business, and what if the publisher tries to cheat you?

Let's talk about literary agents (or representatives) a bit so you can decide for yourself which is the best way to go.

In the alleged good old days—before WW II—literary representatives generally had an excellent education, a sincere love of words and literature, an understanding of how the publishing industry functions, and a congenial manner. That was before the paperback revolution, when editors and publishers also had these qualities, and the publication of good literature was more important than profits. The aim was to encourage writing talent; even if the first book or two lost money, agents and editors and publishers had faith in the writer's abilities. Enough faith to put up with slow sales or even a dud.

I was a kid during World War II. The only paperbacks I'd ever seen were the Armed Forces editions of popular hardcover books. And then Pocket Books (the very first *successful* paperback company . . . though there have been paperbacks in this country since the Civil War) burst upon the scene. I read James Hilton's *Lost Horizon* and Pearl Buck's *The Good Earth* in paperback. Back then, they didn't varnish the covers; instead, a type of cellophane was affixed to the cover, and had a most irritating way of curling at the edges, like the peeling of a sunburn. And I became hooked on reading. I could afford the books out of my allowance, and I didn't have to take them back to the library on time or face a fine. The paperback business has come a very long way since then!

There is no college or university that gives a diploma on how to be an agent, or an editor, or a publisher. It's a seat-of-the-pants business; though some few colleges are now conducting seminars or special courses (one offers a certificate in publishing) about specific aspects of the business, you still can't get a degree in it. You get a job, and you learn.

How does this affect you, as author? Simple. You are going to be dealing with individuals, not clearly defined company policy; you will be subject to each individual's personal whim, opinion, and extent of learning. There is no right or wrong—only subjective reaction that one *hopes* is based on expertise and open-mindedness. Yet, if an agent has a rotten cold, or the editor was just told to shape up or ship out . . . these influences can and do frequently determine how either will look at your work.

I have been a published writer, a book editor on salary, and an agent. Believe me when I say that this is a business that depends largely on the frames of mind of the people who read your work. Unlike the auto parts business (if you need a muffler, you need a muffler), you are going to try to sell your "creation." Its reception will vary depending on whether the agent has gout, or the editor just got a raise in pay, or any of the other daily events that shape a person's emotions and attitudes. If you are not prepared to accept this, you are in for a lot of shattering disappointment.

Well may you ask: "You mean, after I spend months and months of working, honing, rewriting, polishing . . . that my book may or may not be accepted on the basis of digestion?"

Answer: "Yes." That's the bad news.

The good, though, is that almost everyone in this business has had years and years of experience and knows it if it's a good day to read manuscripts for evaluation, or to put it off till another day. More importantly, when you "read for a living" (as agents and editors do), you acquire the expertise to swiftly spot a good or a bad manuscript in very short order.

There's an anecdote told about the late Bennett Cerf. Apparently, one of his readers at Random House returned a submission with a standard rejection form. The author, irate, wrote directly to Mr. Cerf in protest.

Dear Mr. Cerf:
I was aghast at the return of my manuscript when it wasn't
even given a complete reading. I *know* no one there read the
entire book because I stapled some of the pages together before
sending it to you. It came back with the pages still stapled!

As gossip has it, the letter went on and on in furious indignation. And as
the story goes, Mr. Cerf allegedly wrote back: "My dear sir . . . one
does not have to eat the whole egg to know that it is rotten."

While that wasn't very nice of Mr. Cerf, if you knew how many
weird submissions publishers receive, you'd understand his side of the
story, too.

Dealing with agents isn't too terribly different. They, too, receive
dozens and dozens of unrequested manuscripts every week. And
whether you like the idea or not, a lot of writers are just downright
crazy—which makes it harder for the rest of us. They'll phone agents in
the middle of the night, try to trap them as they leave a restaurant, and
are more persistent than a terrier. Writers can have awesome egos, and
this definitely puts them in the TBA class—To Be Avoided.

One of my favorite stories that illustrates the egocentricity of
writers is about the famous author at a very chi-chi New York City
cocktail party. He'd cornered a sympathetic-looking young woman, and
for more than an hour talked of nothing else but his writing career.
Finally sensing that she was becoming bored, he said: "But let's not talk
about me anymore—let's talk about *you!* What did you think of my latest
book?"

An agent is a psychologist, a bill collector, a moderator, a confi-
dante, and a salesperson. If agents are connected with large agencies,
they may be on salary or draw against commission. If they are self-
employed, their livelihood depends on their judgment about a book, and
the ability to sell it. Books that do not sell do not earn an agent's
commission; and agents have hefty overhead expenses, especially in
New York City. Anyone can become a literary agent; not anyone can
made a decent living at it.

This should tell you something. In plain language, that no agent is
going to represent your work unless he or she believes it can be sold to a
publisher. Yet again, do not forget that this decision can be subjective. If
an agent declines to represent your work, it could well be an agent who is
unable to see its merits . . . not that your work isn't any good.

Traditionally, an agent never charged a reading fee; wasn't so
concerned if you'd been published before or not; submitted manuscripts
to editors with a polite note expressing hope that the editor would find it
suitable for his or her list; and if the book sold, took ten percent off the
top of any monies the book received (inclusive of magazine serialization,
movie rights, book club rights, and so on). Agents spent a reasonable

amount of time lunching with authors and editors, or going to cocktail parties—all of it pure business, not for fun.

Things are changing. Not radically, but changing. More agents are beginning to charge reading fees—particularly if you've never before been published. (While it's not standard practice yet, I have to agree that agents spend an awful lot of time reading pure unsalable junk—they're entitled to a fee.) Many of them will apply this fee against the earnings of the book, so in the long run the author paid nothing. Be sure to ask, before agreeing to be represented, what the agent's stance is on this point.

Some agents simply refuse to represent an unpublished writer; they won't even read your work "just in case." Some will consider representing partial manuscripts; others will not. Their rules and regulations differ and are usually rooted in personal experiences with writers, and editors.

There is also a swing toward charging a fifteen percent commission for domestic sales; it's standard for agents to charge twenty-five percent for foreign sales because they usually have to split the commission with a foreign representative.

And some agents are telling authors what to write, making demands upon writers to revise to their specifications. With rare exception, I am very much against this practice. An agent is not a writer . . . nor, in all likelihood, an editor. If an editor wants me to change my novel, I am very glad to do so; however, the editor is the one who will be *buying* the book—not the agent. Since agents do not purchase manuscripts for publication, but sell them, I am leery of agents who tell writers how to write. On the other hand, if my agent makes suggestions that I can readily see would improve my book, then I'd have to be insane to refuse.

A reasonable question to ask is: "So what do I get for the ten or fifteen percent commission?"

Technically, you *should* get someone who knows the business well; who is on a friendly basis with as many editors as possible; and who has stayed on top of which publisher is looking for what, new trends in the making, and so forth. Some agents keep apprised of what's happening in the motion picture and television industries; and some have co-agents through whom they work. A good agent should be able to read your manuscript and know that it is, for instance, too sophisticated for Silhouette Books . . . yet might very well fit in with Silhouette's longer books provided you expand it.

At that point, the agent will be in touch with you to give you your options. He or she may telephone the editor at Silhouette to say that though the manuscript needs to be fleshed out, perhaps the editor would like to see it anyway. Or—especially if you've never sold before—the agent may insist on receiving the additional material first, just to be absolutely certain you really can do it.

Once the sale to a publisher is made, and depending upon the terms of the contract, a good agent will pursue subsidiary rights (see Glossary), and in every other way nurse your novel along until nothing more can be done for it. In reality, most romances never see any additional monies other than what they earn in paperback book form. Don't expect the book to have a big movie sale or to become a book-club selection. There are simply too many romances to choose from, and in truth, few are well-written enough to warrant any additional sales.

These are the things you should expect when you have a good agent. But remember that I said anybody can become an agent? That's where you've got to be on your guard. There are a disconcerting number of people who have set themselves up as literary agents . . . and they don't know the first thing about the business. I've even met agents who cannot comprehend a contract, who can't tell a good book from a bad one, and—to all intents and purposes—are little more than a mailroom clearing house for unsuspecting authors. Granted, the inept ones are in the minority—but they do exist.

I met an agent once—thank the fates, only once—who had a genuine scam going. It was legal, but immoral and unethical as all blazes. To avoid a lawsuit, I'll call this agent "it" instead of "he" or "she." It would receive submissions of manuscripts from hopeful authors. It had proper stationery, offices, a secretary, and so forth—there was no way for anyone to assume anything other than a legitimate business operation. However, whenever it could get away with it, it would tell an author that his or her work really wasn't salable . . . but, that it would be willing to *buy* the manuscript and take a chance, absorbing the loss should it fail to sell the work elsewhere. Well, naturally, a lot of writers fell for this; they were thrilled to make a sale of any kind. The twist? It would then put a new title page on the manuscript, with its own name as author, and sell it to a regular publisher (having first acquired a bill of sale, all very legal, from the original author). So for an outlay of anywhere from $50.00 to $500.00, it kept all the profits for itself plus getting the credit of authorship!

Be leery of agents who ask you to "sign up" with them. Most established agents accept that the agent–author relationship is more of an affair than a marriage. It is ridiculous to legally tie an author to an agent if that author isn't happy. Unhappy writers rarely produce salable books, so agents let the author go ("unhappy" in the sense of with one's agent, not emotionally despondent). However, there's another side to that coin, too. All too frequently, agents encourage their writers nobly; they spend hours on the telephone, write lengthy letters, and really work at making a sale.

This type of bolstering is a very definite expense for agents. What occurs too frequently, though, is that after an author finally becomes a big success, that writer will dump the original agent in favor of someone with more posh offices, a bigger name, or whatever. Not fair; not fair at all. Yet, the majority of established agents still do not require any binding agreement to be signed.

How can you tell a good agent from a bad one? You can't. Not really. While it would be easy to say that you should stick to those agents who have been around for a long time, that would be grossly unfair to new agents who might be every bit as competent, if not more so. (For that matter, old-time agents might be slowing up or getting bored.) It would also be a disservice to state that agents in New York City are superior to those in smaller cities. I've known several agents across the country—some of whom have never even been to New York—who make very comfortable livings, and do quite well by their authors. However, I must admit to a certain amount of prejudice; agents who are based in New York City have greater access to editors, and it is therefore (presumably) more likely that they will know what editors are looking for. There's no guarantee of that, naturally.

Well, then, how *do* you select an agent! If you can't have one recommended to you, it's no different from finding a good physician. Open up the Yellow Pages, close your eyes and see where your finger lands. That's one way. Another is to spend some time at your local public library and each week read Paul S. Nathan's column in *Publishers Weekly*. This is the publishing industry's official source of weekly information, and most libraries subscribe. If you're very nice, the librarian may let you read it as long as it's on the premises. While this column cannot possibly cover every single sale that is made, you will begin to notice that certain agents' names appear more frequently than others—a sale here, a deal there. Maybe those agents aren't people with whom you'd ever want to be friends, but they're making sales—and that's the bottom line, after all.

A good agent should be able to negotiate a contract in your favor. However, in the romance market, there is very little latitude about negotiating clauses. Some few concessions may be made if the book is head and shoulders above other submissions, but the concessions may not be enough to really brag about. For the most part, category fiction isn't subject to a lot of wheeling and dealing. Editors have been given ceilings on what they can pay authors, and if an agent begins to insist on a change in this clause, and striking out that clause, an editor is just as likely to say "no thanks." They receive hundreds of romances from hopeful writers who don't care what the contract says at all as long as their books are accepted for publication.

However, let's say you've found that good agent and your romance has been sold. The contracts are all signed and you have a copy for your files. Your agent will—if you're short of money—do a bit of nagging at the publisher's accounting department to hurry that check along. And when it's time for your royalty accounting, your agent will see to it that there's no unreasonable delay; and if monies are due to you, **nag** accounting again. (Accounting departments in the publishing business suffer from a notorious reputation for dragging their heels. I've never found out if it's truly warranted across the board; but I've worked at some publishing companies where I swore accounting was jealous of writers, arbitrarily withholding checks when they were overdue.)

Do not think that because you have an agent you are going to be best friends, even if you live next door to each other. Your agent is a business associate, not your chum, and you are *not* your agent's only client! Be as businesslike as is humanly possible, taking your lead from the agent for deportment. Don't start getting cute, sending birthday cards or trinkets of appreciation—unless you'd do the same thing for your dentist or auto mechanic.

All right, so what happens if you decide not to have an agent at all. Surprise: There are many editors who actually prefer to deal directly with authors, eliminating the middleman. This is particularly true with category fiction such as romances.

Let's face it. This is your very first novel—are you going to nitpick over the contract? In all likelihood, you won't even know what you're signing! Fortunately, crooked editors or publishers are the exception, not the rule. One of the easiest ways to spot a crooked editor is if he or she tells you that your romance is a borderline situation for acceptance, but for ten percent (or any kind of sum) the editor will tip the balance in your favor. Ye olde kickback, plain and simple. Get your manuscript back as quickly as you can—though taking pains not to anger the editor. Angry, crooked editors have been known to do very nasty things—like besmirch your reputation, "lose" your manuscript in the wastebasket, and so forth.

I cannot overemphasize how unlikely it is that you'll run into this type of person. With roughly twenty years in this business, I've only heard of two editors like that, both of whom have been run out of the business. Publishing is a pretty small clique, and word gets around very quickly.

Some beginning writers worry unduly that an editor will steal their ideas. First, as I've said before, the new copyright law protects your novel the moment it's finished. Second, very few editors are also writers. It is much more likely that another writer will steal your novel after it's been published. Broke, despondent, with families to support, writers have been known to plagiarize other people's books. And in a field as crowded as romances, you'd probably never know it even if someone stole your story.

But let's say you find out. A novel of mine was plagiarized and the only way I learned of it was because a reader wrote me a blasting letter, bawling me out for pulling such a shoddy trick as merely changing the title, the names of the characters and the locale, then selling exactly the same novel to some other publisher. I hadn't the faintest idea of what she was talking about and asked her to tell me what the title was, and who published it. The irate reader calmed down, and very kindly sent me the copy of the book she'd purchased. Yup. Word for word—the same novel, except for the changes noted above.

Some fellow in Texas had bought my novel, copied it on his typewriter, and submitted it to a hole-in-the-wall paperback publisher in the Midwest. I don't know about the laws today, but back then, if I wanted to sue, I would have had to establish residence in Texas. The guy was paid a mere $500.00 for the novel, and the publisher was so small that none of it was worth pursuing. All I was able to do was force the publisher to withdraw the plagiarized version from sale. Frankly, anyone who would stoop to such a thing has to be in desperate straits. However, I never forgot his name, and since I am also an editor, our paths crossed once more. He made the mistake of submitting a manuscript to the company where I worked. It was ten years later, but I still hadn't forgotten. I saw his cover letter and the pseudonym he was using, and quickly scrawled off a note: "Who'd you steal this one from?" His manuscript was returned—unread. That may sound rather petty, but you'll understand should it ever happen to you.

You should bear in mind that romances are written to a specific formula. If you decide to write a romance with bullfighting as the backdrop . . . don't you think that there are at least a dozen other authors who've also had the same idea? Nobody "stole" your concept. It's a matter of the odds that with so many people writing for the romance market, ideas will and do overlap. So if I've set you up for a first-rate case of paranoia, you can relax.

Let's go back to what happens if you're unagented. You had already decided that your romance was going to be for Silhouette Books. Obviously, that's where you start. You can go one of two ways: (1) Send a query letter first to inquire if the editor is interested in seeing it; or (2) just send it in cold turkey—what we call "over the transom" submissions. Sometimes a publisher's guidelines will tell you the preferred way of handling this; sometimes not.

I have found that most editors—myself included—prefer the query letter, generally accompanied by a *brief* outline of the novel. This saves me time, shelf space, and alerts me to the fact that the author may well have something better than I might have expected (an unusual plot, a background that is not overworked, or the heroine has an interesting career and the author seems to know a great deal about that business).

Query letters are also in *your* best interest:

(1) There is no rule about how many editors you can send query letters to; if you think your romance might fit just as well in some other publisher's line, it's perfectly all right to send a letter to them as well.

However, there is a *firm* rule against submitting your manuscript to more than one editor at a time! Never do that—if your agent wants to, okay; but not you!

(2) If the editor says yes, and you send your manuscript along, return postage is on the publisher. If you send in the manuscript "over the transom," you must enclose a self-addressed stamped envelope suitable for returning your work.

(3) Time. An editor can answer your letter in a matter of days; but if your manuscript has to be read first, it can be months and months and months.

The query letter.   Why it should be so, I don't know—other than the fact that the act of writing a letter is becoming a dying art; however, most writers are scared silly of the query letter. It's fundamentally simple; and the simpler you keep it, the better.

It should be typed single-space; a handwritten letter will probably be thrown away since it shows that the writer is an amateur who hasn't taken the trouble to find out some of the basic etiquette of publishing practices. The letter should be free from error. Why? Well, look at it from the editor's point of view . . . if just a letter has a lot of strikeovers and mistakes, God knows what your manuscript will look like! Consequently, the neater and more professional your letter, the more receptive an editor will be.

The query letter should be brief. If humanly possible, confine it to just *one* page; all it has to do is introduce who you are, and why you are writing to the editor. The editor doesn't give a darn how many children you have, what your husband does, or how talented your mother thinks you are. Just the facts that pertain to the reason for writing and nothing more.

A query letter, then, is nothing more than a request for permission to submit your manuscript. It should be calm, reasonable, un-cute, and if you have any special qualifications, include them. In this example, it was computer technology; but if you've worked in a veterinarian's office, the mortgage department of a bank, or any other area that you are using for a background, it's important to tell the editor. (Many writers of romances invent interesting careers for their heroines and then fail to tell the reader anything about this side of the heroine's life . . . probably because the author knows nothing about that profession.)

Whatever you can bring to the query letter that helps to sell your romance—without giving yourself hickies for excellence—should be part of the query letter.

As stated in the letter, enclose a Xerox copy (not the original) of a two- or three-page synopsis of your novel. If you need five pages . . . okay, but try to avoid anything more than that. Shorter is faster—therefore, better.

A typical query letter might go as follows:

> Jane Doe
> xxx Main Street
> Centerville, U.S.A.
> (date)
>
> Karen Solem
> Editor-in-Chief
> Silhouette Romances
> 1230 Avenue of the Americas
> New York, New York 10020
>
> Dear Ms. Solem:
>
> As an avid reader of your line of romances, I have written a romance of my own entitled: <u>Romance Of My Own</u>. I have perused your guidelines and believe that my novel fits your requirements.
>
> Set in Lower Slobovia, it is the story of a young American woman on an exchange program for computer technologists. Mary Smith, the heroine, is instantly attracted to the American manager of her division, Greg Super; however, he seems to resent her presence and she cannot figure out why. A more detailed outline is enclosed for your convenience.
>
> The completed manuscript is estimated at 58,500 words. May I point out, Ms. Solem, that I have worked in computer technology and know my subject well. Consequently, the background information is completely authentic and with so many women going into this field, I believe readers will find added interest as a result of the background.
>
> I should very much like to submit <u>Romance Of My Own</u> to you, and look forward to your reply. In the interim, thank you for your consideration.
>
> Sincerely,
>
> Jane Doe

If, however, you are asking the editor's permission to submit a partial manuscript (what it sounds like—incomplete), then the letter will have to be altered slightly. Obviously, you will not say "complete" nor the estimated word count. Instead, you will talk about "my manuscript in progress, of which I now have the opening four chapters completed" and address yourself to the book's "projected length of between 55–60,000 words." You will, of course, still enclose the synopsis.

A word or so about submitting partial manuscripts. Many writers do not understand how to go about this. I have received "submissions" of a single, random page from each chapter of a book; or the fifth and seventh chapters, but nothing else; and so on. An editor can tell nothing from this type of submission other than that you're not a pro.

If you intend to submit a partial manuscript, send the *opening* chapters, complete and in sequence. Otherwise, it's like walking into the theater during the middle of the movie; the viewer can't tell who's who, what went before, why this scene should matter, and so forth. If at all possible, send at least five or six chapters; but never less than three.

Over-the-transom submissions. Whether a partial or a complete manuscript, it will still require a cover letter (which, as far as I'm concerned, means you might just as well have sent the query letter and saved time). The cover letter should say everything the query letter does, except that you're not asking if it's all right to submit . . . you've submitted.

Again, do *not* send suggested artwork for the cover. It is a good idea, however, to enclose a synopsis even with a completed manuscript: It saves the editor time. It's not imperative, but it's helpful.

Your manuscript should be sent in a sturdy box or in a padded mailing bag. It does not have to be bound in any way other than by a couple of rubber bands.

I have bought many an author's manuscript without an agent being involved; so have dozens of other editors. If you become a big-time writer (another Janet Dailey, for instance), then the need for an agent is obvious. Though you may also wish to look into attorneys' firms that represent authors; there's a growing number of them.

For the most part, though, you will be so thrilled that an editor is willing to actually pay you for your romance, that your name will be on the cover, and the book will be published . . . you really don't have to have an agent at this point in your career. The decision is yours, of course; I simply think it a waste of money to pay a commission to someone when there is no likelihood of negotiating a contract.

A word of warning: If you decide to submit directly, do *not* bring in an agent to conclude the deal! Nothing turns an editor off faster, and you may find yourself with no sale at all. Bringing an agent in on a deal after discussions have begun (you don't even have to have reached the contract stage—just discussions) is like springing your mother on your groom as a come-along on the honeymoon. Don't do it! You began the whole process; you finish it. Should you happen to acquire an agent in the interim, then that person should handle your *next* book . . . not this one.

What you must be prepared for, agented or otherwise, is waiting. You will do an unbearable amount of that. Why? Because of the sheer volume of manuscripts agents and editors receive, and the amazing number of problems that seem to automatically come along with writers: They can't meet their deadlines because of a broken wrist, breakup with a lover, it's tax time—you name it, editors and agents have heard it all.

Before submitting to a publishing company, take the time to find out who the editor in charge is, the correct spelling of that editor's name, and title. All of this can be gleaned from an annual directory called *Literary Market Place* (published by R. R. Bowker, the same publishers of *Publishers Weekly*). Your local public library will probably have a copy; if not, try the largest book store nearest to where you live.

Should you want to buy one for your own personal use, write to: R. R. Bowker Company, 1180 Avenue of the Americas, New York, NY 10036. They are expensive; worse, editors move about quite a bit, so frequently *LMP* (as it's known in the industry) is outdated before it's been bound. Because publishing companies are renowned for their niggardly attitudes towards editors' salaries, very often the only way an editor can get a raise in pay is to move to a different company. Publishers are far more inclined to give their editors a fancy new title rather than an increase in salary; titles do not pay the rent.

Because of this, however, it is now very difficult to tell just who's in charge of what. Editorial Director, Executive Editor, Senior Editor, and so on; I'm rapidly reaching the point where I believe that the publishing industry should convert to a system of military rank. At least a person could figure out just who the head honcho is!

If you're going through an agent, you must wait for him or her to get around to your manuscript. Then, there's the period of each of you sorting through realistic expectations, how the agent operates and so forth. Once this is all agreed to, your manuscript is sent to a publisher. And now you begin to wait in earnest—I've waited as much as a *year* for a decision from an editor. In fact, I've frequently nattered on that no one should be hired as an editor until that individual has spent two years—without outside income or help—as a writer. It'll never happen, of course; but at least editors would come to understand just how awful it is to *wait*.

Then there's their side of the story. . . .

The Editor's Side
of the Desk

Whatever most of you think is typical of a paperback editor's day at the office, forget it. They are the most grossly underpaid, and creative, people in America; they are also frequently overworked and pressured.

Generally, their offices are woefully small, often windowless, with never enough bookshelves or tables; their desks are almost always a complete mess. Do not be deceived; *they* know precisely where everything is. They have to—there's nowhere else to put anything.

It's Monday morning. Edna Editor has just climbed two flights of stairs from the subway, battled by shouldering through the thousands of people also three minutes late to work, yet strives for a cheerful "good morning" to her co-workers. Edna Editor is in charge of her division of the paperback company: Raging Romances.

She may have a secretary; she might not. However, Edna is responsible for seeing four romances per month to press, so she will have an editorial assistant (be the title associate, or senior—it's help, and Edna needs all the help she can get). For only four books per month? You better believe it.

Unlike hardcover houses that have "seasons" (the fall list, the spring list, etc.) and infinitely fewer books to publish per year, paperback houses operate on very tight monthly schedules, *simultaneously* working on as many as six months' worth of books at a time! For those of you who are genuinely interested in this, I'm including in this chapter a copy of how I set up my own editorial working schedule for ease of reference. Once a book is put into schedule for publication, it gets preference over everything else.

In the paperback business, the covers have to be run off well in advance of the book going to press; generally, about five or six months ahead of the book's actual publication date. And all the covers for all the books in that month's list must be done and sent off to the production department at the same time (give or take a couple of days).

What does this mean? (1) Edna must have completely read all four manuscripts for that month. (2) She will prepare a list of alternate titles—either for committee approval, or her immediate boss's. Paperback companies love to change titles; usually they're quite right. When my hardcover novel *Bequeath Them No Tumbled House* was bought for reprint, I was grateful when the title was changed to *Deadly Legacy*. Authors, even old hands, are rarely objective about their own work. Then, too, there's the matter of a romance already published with that same title you provided; or a romance on Edna's list of forthcoming titles that is either the same, or too close. Do not be surprised if the title of your book is changed. (3) Jacket copy—sometimes called "blurbs," though that's technically erroneous—must be written for front and back covers, plus the front sales (page one, where a scene from the book is condensed, beefed up, or otherwise altered to better interest a prospective buyer). (4) A synopsis of the story must be written at the same time, along with any salient information that would prove beneficial to the sales force—unless Edna is lucky enough to have a publicity department to do that for her. (5) Edna must also come up with ideas for the art department on how to illustrate the book. It's rare that the art department will follow her suggestions, but she has to do it anyway.

Remember that this is for four books simultaneously. While she's doing this, she will be: (1) copyediting manuscripts due to the production department; (2) proofreading manuscripts set into type; (3) checking the signatures before the book is printed and bound.

In the meantime: Edna is answering correspondence and telephone calls from agents, authors, her boss, questions from other departments, and making lunch dates with magazine editors, going to editorial and production meetings, and if she can find four minutes to make an appointment with her dentist, she's lucky!

Then, Edna has to meet with you while you're in town, along with other authors on her lists, and make each of you feel very welcome and special—never mind that she can't see you over the clutter on her desk. While you're there, a writer telephones to complain that her contracts haven't been received. That writer is placed on "hold" while Edna calls the legal department; or if it's a complaint about not receiving a check, she'll call the accounting department.

As if all this weren't enough, there's that table over there with dozens and dozens of solicited and unsolicited manuscripts to be evaluated. I have found that it takes reading about twenty submissions to find one I can accept. Mind you, romance editors *want* to accept your work; they are desperate to feed the voracious schedule they must meet. Nothing would make them happier than if they could accept every manuscript they read—but it doesn't happen that way. Everybody *wants* to be a writer; few people are (that's the whole purpose of this book . . . to help you!).

As you already know, Edna is an overworked person. It will take time for her to get to your romance. If you want to avoid wondering whether or not your manuscript ever got to Raging Romances, enclose a self-addressed postcard with your manuscript. On it, write a brief message such as:

> Your romance entitled_____ (title)
> was received this date_____.
> (Leave this part blank so Edna can fill it in.) Please allow _____ weeks before expecting a decision from us. (Again, blank so Edna can give you a ballpark idea of when she might get around to your book. Then leave enough space so Edna can sign her name, or use a Raging Romance rubber stamp.)

If you don't enclose a manuscript-received postcard, it is traditional to allow at least eight weeks before you send a *polite* inquiry about its status. Ideally, in today's rush, give Edna ten weeks before you make any inquiries. An agent can generally give a call after about six weeks, yet agents know how very busy editors are and try not to be nags.

If you remember nothing else, keep in mind that there are thousands of writers wanting their romances to be published. If you antagonize your editor, you will lose the sale no matter how good your romance might be! The last thing in the world an editor needs is an overanxious or wheedling writer! And just to reinforce just how strange some writers are, I once received an eight-by-ten-inch glossy photograph—a typical "author's" photograph, heavily shadowed and posed. There was no letter with the photo, but on the back of it, the man had written:

> This is my formal author's photograph. You will never be able to use it because I wouldn't dream of sending you my novel. It's much too good for the company you work for. All editors are jerks in the first place and would not be able to appreciate what a superior writer I am.

It wasn't signed; there was no return address. What was I supposed to do with it? Naturally, it was thrown away with a shake of the head.

All right, Edna finally gets around to reading your romance. It's been on that table for anywhere from three to six or seven months. Most editors date the manuscripts when they come in and try to read them in order of arrival. She reads your romance and loves it. She must now write to you and tell you that she is interested in contracting for your work. Maybe it needs some revisions—are you willing to do them? For that matter, are you capable of doing them? (Not all writers can revise their work; and some simply refuse to do so. At that point, Edna may well have wasted her time reading your manuscript; and if you ever submit to her again, no matter where she's working, she'll probably remember your name and reject the manuscript outright. There's no point in reading a writer's work if that writer is a known uncooperative person.) This is equally true for not submitting your manuscript to another editor at the same time. If Edna reads it, then finds out you've sold it to some other editor—well, I wouldn't want to be in your shoes!

But you're a knowledgeable person after reading this book, and you know that revisions may well be expected of you. So you listen to (or read) what it is Edna wants changed, and you agree to do it. A modicum of *polite* disagreement is permissible, but don't forget this is your very first sale—don't alienate Edna, who already has plenty of problems. If you genuinely don't like the requested changes (and give them some time to filter down so you don't argue needlessly), then make two or three counter-suggestions. This will show Edna that you are not a "deathless prose writer" (nothing can be worse!), and that you're fully willing to cooperate with her for the betterment of the book . . . only that you have a few ideas of your own. Most editors will compromise if they possibly can. They still have to meet those schedules, and they must have manuscripts to do so. Some will remain adamant about what changes are required, and that's that.

So you've now agreed on the changes. This is *not* a guarantee of a sale to Edna. She first has to be sure you really can do it. Naturally, *you* are confident that you can, and your husband sweetly offers to cook dinner for two weeks while you work on your revisions, and your oldest son says he'll do the laundry. Dusting and vacuuming can wait (unless you can assign the tasks to your other children). If you live alone, nothing matters as much as rewriting your romance to please Edna.

The revisions are done, and you send them off to Edna. At this point, she will make a genuine effort to get to them as quickly as possible. Not only is Edna a considerate individual, but she *has* to buy manuscripts for publication, or have gaps in her schedule . . . and probably lose her job. And Edna is very anxious to find out if you've pulled off the changes satisfactorily so she can send you a contract. If the company where she works has a legal department, they'll take care of that (after she tells them what terms were negotiated or if it's a standard contract); if there isn't a legal department, then that's just one more duty Edna has to perform. (I sincerely hope that every editor who reads this book will show this chapter to her or his boss and ask for a raise!)

You've done your work well and Edna sends you her company's standard contractual agreement. A few weeks later, you'll probably receive an Author's Questionnaire. (Not all paperback houses do this, however.) Fill it out and return it as quickly as you can, and be sure to avoid laboriously long answers.

You have now delivered your baby, and have turned it over to an adoption agency. From this moment on, you have *nothing* more to do with your romance! That's it. It's over. You've done your part, now the adoption agency will do its.

Hard Facts

You have no say in a title change.

You will not be consulted about the sell-copy on the jacket, or the illustration.

You will not be taken out to lunch unless your book will be Edna's lead title, or because she's very nice, or because she wants to encourage you to submit more manuscripts.

You will have nothing to do with the style of the body of the book nor with minor editorial changes.

You will not appear on television talkshows, or have a national author's tour—unless your book really sells exceptionally well, or the publisher's faith in it warrants such an expensive push.

It will probably be at least a year before your book is published; often, longer. Smaller companies may go to press in less time, but most of the romance publishers work far, far in advance.

Now what? If Edna's schedule is on time, and she has a sufficient number of manuscripts on hand for the moment, your romance will be placed on a special shelf, table, or whatever, along with other contracted-for manuscripts. (By the way, when your contracts arrive, they will have no signatures on them. You're expected to sign your copies, send them back, and then an authorized individual from the company will sign a copy, and return that executed copy to you for your files. This can take anywhere from two to ten weeks. Be patient.)

To back up for a moment, let me explain a bit about some of the words I'm throwing around as if everyone knew what I meant. (They'll appear again in the Glossary for ready reference.)

In large companies, with big payrolls, employees tend to become compartmentalized and perform the same specific job over and over; the books may be different, but the duties are not. An editor edits, a copyeditor copyedits and so on; some companies have specialists in writing jacket copy, some do not. However, we've set up Raging Romance with just Edna and her editorial associate or assistant. This means the two of them must do just about everything without help.

Editing. This is when you read the manuscript for content. Is it well written? Does the story line make sense? Are the characters believable? Has the author thrown away a scene that could be infinitely more powerful? In short, "editing" is reading the manuscript to find out if the overall premise works and is entertaining for the market it appeals to. Little or no attention is paid to grammar, misspellings and so forth.

Copyediting. You need good eyes, a superb memory, and a love for detail. This is where you try to catch all the author's mistakes and correct them on the manuscript itself. Sometimes the copyeditor will spot a detail or concept that seems doubtful or questionable, and will flag that line to double-check with the author or the editor.

Proofreading. Once the manuscript has been edited and copyedited, it can go back to Edna for verification of the copyeditor's questions, or to the author, or both. All that taken care of and everyone is happy, it goes to the production department. There it is set into type.

If the printer uses computer typesetting methods, Edna will receive a copy of the "repros." Otherwise, she'll get a set of "galleys." Repros is short for "reproductions." It means that all the typeset information has already been pasted down on oblong pieces of cardboard, paginated, just as the final book will be printed. Edna will get a Xerox copy of these; hence, "repros." "Galleys" refer to very long, narrow sheets of paper where the text of the book has been printed with continuous lines of type; no page numbers, no resemblance to how the published book will actually look.

Printers make mistakes. No matter how excellent they are, they will still make mistakes. Sometimes paragraphs can be left out, even a chapter. I once worked at a publishing firm that used a printing company more accustomed to girlie magazines than paperback books. I was proofreading a Western novel and there was (of course) the scene where the Indians had raided a community of settlers. The lieutenant had ridden his horse all night to tell the fort's commander. The line from the book should have been: " 'Send for the messenger,' the commander barked." However, when I received the repros to double-check, the line read: " 'Send for the massagers,' the commander barked." You've got to watch printers.

So either repros or galleys have to be proofread by Edna or her associate. This is their last chance to catch any errors a printer may have made; or oversights of their own.

Signature (brownline or blueline). A signature is thirty-two sequential pages of the book; signatures are later bound together, not individual pages. With computerized printers, Edna will receive "brownlines" or "bluelines." As far as Edna, her associate, and you are concerned, they're basically the same thing as signatures.

These must be checked *in case,* between galley or repro, and signature/brownline, pages have been transposed, chapters have fallen out, or large portions pasted upside down. I once worked on a nonfiction book that continually referred to a specific chart. Throughout all the checks and counterchecks, not I, my boss, the author, or the printer caught the fact that the chart had been omitted at the typesetting stage. The book was published, and then had to be recalled from retailers. Another company I worked at did an updated edition of a highly successful cookbook (fortunately, I wasn't involved with that fiasco). When it was published, it turned out that the ingredients for recipes had been transposed with the others, and none of the ingredients applied to the recipes. The authors sued—and won.

So when we talk about proofreading, we mean making sure that the typesetter has set the manuscript as it was supposed to be, without error (some always will slip by the editor or author), and that the book is as perfect as it can be.

On the other hand, maybe Edna needs to fill a slot in her schedule and your book is it. Let's say it's now October. Edna is working on galleys and signatures for the December list of books; getting copyedited manuscripts to production for the January list; and completing all cover information for the April list. Let's also assume she has slotted your romance to be a May title. Cover information won't be due to the art department until next month—November of this year.

Why are the covers done first? So the salesmen can be taking advance orders from book retailers, using the covers (and any other information the company may supply, such as you being a local author or somesuch) for "show and tell" purposes. And why is this important? Funny you should ask. It's so the publisher can estimate how many copies of your book to print. Paper must be ordered, press time re-

served, costs projected and a host of other factors—most of which will
have an effect on how many copies of your book should be printed. If
there's, for instance, retailer resistance (for *whatever* reason), fewer
copies will be printed.

The reason for this is simple. Paperbacks are sold on consignment to
retailers. Any copies not sold within a given period of time will be
returned to the publisher for a full credit. Overestimating the sale of your
book can cost the publisher a small fortune. And what's he or she
supposed to do with the returned copies? Warehousing is expensive, and
there's not enough catsup in the world to just eat them. For this reason,
some publishers ask retailers to return only the cover from the book,
torn off from the spine. It saves shipping and warehousing costs; it also
means that there's not a chance in the world that your book might be sent
out to secondary retail outlets. While that's not good news for you, many
in this business consider it only sound economics. If your book isn't
selling, get rid of it and swallow the losses.

Now then, back to the editorial side, and your book. Bear in mind
that it is now October and look at the schedule Edna has to work with.
Her department is all through with Raging Romances' list of books
through November, and almost everything has been taken care of for the
December lists. (Not all publishers have such tight schedules, by the
way, but this will at least give you a very good idea of what kind of
pressure Edna is under.)

"No." refers to the books' numbers (dropping off the ISBN prefix—
ISBN stands for International Standard Book Number, useful to librarians and retailers). "Title" is obvious. "Due" refers to when Edna must
have that portion of the process completed in order to meet deadline;
"actual" refers to when she really turned it in (no cheating, either!). I
find this kind of chart easiest for me. I can pace my own work, predict
areas of possible panic and keep tabs on how my department is doing.
Edna doubtlessly has one quite similar to this, and can tell at a glance
what's due when, and if she's ahead of schedule or behind. (And you
thought all we did was read manuscripts and have lavish luncheons!)

As you can quickly see, when it comes to editorial deadlines, Edna
is pretty on top of things. Something must have happened this October,
though, because she was late with all her April cover information.
Perhaps she was out with a cold, or nobody liked what she presented so
she had to do it all over again. However, once that manuscript is sent to
the typesetter, Edna is now subject to pressures from that department,
along with whatever else might go wrong in her own department. As you
can see for December's titles, the production department was very slow
in getting those proofs to her; and with one book, even though it was due
to Edna with sufficient time for her to proofread and get the proofs back
to production by September 27th . . . production still hasn't given her

Work Schedule: October

No.	Title	COVERS Due	COVERS Actual	MANUSCRIPT Due	MANUSCRIPT Actual	PROOFS Due	PROOFS Actual	REPROS Due	REPROS Actual	BROWNLINES Due	BROWNLINES Actual
	DECEMBER										
3114		6/10	4/28	9/6	8/11	9/27	9/2	10/6	9/14	10/18	
3115		6/10	5/12	9/6	9/2	9/27		10/6		10/18	10/17
3116		6/10	4/27	9/6	8/3	9/27	8/30	10/6	9/3	10/18	
3117		6/10	6/14	9/6	8/16	9/27	9/29	10/6	10/6	10/18	
	JANUARY										
3118		7/9	6/4	10/5	9/29	10/26		11/5		11/16	
3119		7/9	6/4	10/5	9/23	10/26		11/5		11/16	
3120		7/9	6/15	10/5	9/24	10/26		11/5		11/16	
3121		7/9	6/7	10/5	10/1	10/26		11/5		11/16	
	FEBRUARY										
3122		8/10	7/30	11/5		11/24		12/3		12/16	
3123		8/10	7/30	11/5		11/24		12/3		12/16	
3124		8/10	7/29	11/5		11/24		12/3		12/16	
3125		8/10	7/29	11/5		11/24		12/3		12/16	
	MARCH										
3126		9/10	8/30	12/6		12/27		1/5		1/17	
3127		9/10	8/23	12/6		12/27		1/5		1/17	
3128		9/10	8/23	12/6		12/27		1/5		1/17	
3129		9/10	8/23	12/6		12/27		1/5		1/17	
	APRIL										
3130		10/4	10/8	1/5		1/26		2/4		2/18	
3131		10/4	10/8	1/5		1/26		2/4		2/18	
3132		10/4	10/7	1/5		1/26		2/4		2/18	
3133		10/4	10/4	1/5		1/26		2/4		2/18	
	MAY										
3134		11/10		2/5		2/25		3/4		3/14	
3135		11/10		2/5		2/25		3/4		3/14	
3136		11/10		2/5		2/25		3/4		3/14	
3137	YOUR BOOK HERE	11/10		2/5		2/25		3/4		3/14	

the proofs for one title. That means that when they finally do come in, Edna will have to skip a lot of lunches or stay after hours—for which she is *not* paid.

And as you can see, since your book is slotted for May publication, Edna has one month to come up with cover information *while* taking care of everything else in schedule . . . *and* reading manuscripts for possible acceptance.

Now you know why it takes so long to get decisions from editors, and why such emphasis is placed on meeting your deadline. If you don't, and Edna was counting on you, her entire month is thrown off . . . and so is the production department's (they tend to yell a great deal).

Some publishers will send you a Xerox copy of the galleys and ask you to proofread your own book—Edna is also proofing it (or an associate is), but it's a nice courtesy to offer authors when time allows.

Unfortunately, when this happens, writers are given roughly twenty minutes to proofread the entire book and get it back into the mail to Edna. (All right, so that's an exaggeration; however, they never give you *enough* time to be thorough.) If you are asked to proofread your own work, do *not* make any unnecessary changes! If you see a mistake that the copyeditor failed to catch, that's one thing. If Edna cut some of your manuscript (this frequently happens) and it reads poorly, point this out to Edna . . . but don't write on the galleys themselves; use a separate piece of paper. The end of this chapter will provide standard proofreaders' marks for your benefit. Make sure that *all* corrections are in the margins—*never* between the lines.

And for Pete's sake (and Edna's), don't start to rewrite your novel at this stage. It's too late. You should have thought of those additions or deletions before you submitted your final manuscript. It is costly to make changes at this stage, and *you* will be billed for any alterations (called author's alteration or AA's) that didn't appear in the original manuscript. So don't cut, add, or revise now.

If you do, over and beyond the expense, it means the typeset material might not come out right in the published book. Maybe we should discuss the basics of what happens to the manuscript after it's been edited so you can better understand what I mean.

As you've doubtlessly noticed, there are all kinds of different typefaces, and sizes they come in. Some publishers want each book to be "styled" individually; some have a set format. *All* want the final page count of their books to be divisible by thirty-two (paperback companies, not necessarily hardcover). This is because paperbacks are printed thirty-two pages at a time; as explained before, each thirty-two-page section is called a "signature."

Styling a book refers to what typeface is used; how much air there should be between the lines; do chapters begin on right-hand page only, or right or left, or even the middle of a page; is there a "running head" or not (see Glossary); and so forth. Depending on the size of the company, these decisions can be made by the art department; at Raging Romances, Edna will have to choose.

If she asked you for 60,000 words of manuscript, and that's what you gave her, then Edna can pretty well rest assured that—using a particular typeface, margins, etc.—she will have a 176-page printed book. If she wants to run ads in the back of the book, she may have to use a smaller typeface to gain the blank pages, or run the chapters together. Or if you shortchanged her on the word count, you may have a couple of blank pages at the end, or a half title in the front. Blank pages are to be avoided; they cost money whether there's type on them or not. Your publisher is paying for the *paper* either way. (The paper is fed to the printing equipment in sheets large enough for thirty-two typeset pages. One cannot add four extra pages or subtract three. It's going in the equipment prepared for thirty-two pages. Well, one technically *could* add or subtract, but it's prohibitively expensive and unnecessary if you and your editor have done your work properly.)

So once you get your galleys, if you start cutting or changing, that could throw off the number of lines per printed page . . . which, in turn, could wreak havoc with the signature. Theoretically, you could end up with a book that has blank pages between chapters—though production would never permit that to happen. Instead, assuming that Edna had designated that she wanted each chapter to begin on a right-hand page, this might suddenly have to be amended. A most time-consuming and therefore costly process.

Though galleys have not been paginated, it has already been determined how many lines of typeset material will be used for each page. To cut or add is to throw that count off entirely. And that's why any such changes are billed back to the author—it can add up to quite a bit! But again, if it's not your error (you wrote "there" and they typeset "their"), then by all means, indicate the error on the margin. This type of mistake will not be billed back to you. Or, though it happens infrequently, sometimes the typesetter will set the same line twice, drop out a paragraph and so forth. This, too, is not billed back to you. Only your own changes that veer from the original manuscript will be held against you.

However, do not expect to see the galleys. It all depends on which publisher accepts your work, and the individual schedules. As you've already learned, there's very little time to meet all the deadlines, and if the galleys are slow to reach you, lost, or you're late in getting them back to Edna . . . all hell can break loose. It isn't because your publisher isn't considerate; it's only a matter of practicality and time.

So if your picture of an editor was of the tweedy sort, twirling a rose whilst gazing out the window, you now know just how wrong you were.

Oh . . . Edna will have bound copies of your romance sometime in

April. She will send you your free author's copies at that time . . . and you can start bragging that your novel will be on sale in May. "Yes, I'm available for autograph parties—aren't you a dear to ask!"

To Review the Sequence of Events

1) Manuscript received and logged in. This can mean a notebook, or an index card file, or whatever. Your name, title of the manuscript, and the date it was received will be written down.
2) It is placed on what we call "the slush pile." Not very flattering, I agree; but when you've got stacks and stacks of unread manuscripts, all waiting for your attention, that's what it's called.
3) It is ultimately read either by Edna or her associate. If not suitable, it is instantly returned to the author. If it's a "maybe," Edna might ask her associate to read it, too. Final disposition: Yeah, with revisions; or nah, more work than they have the time to give it.
4) Letters or phone calls outlining what terms they are prepared to offer; or explaining what changes will be expected.
5) Copies of the contracts sent to author for signature, and return. An executed copy will be sent to author later.
6) The manuscript is either shelved for future scheduling, or scheduled as soon as possible.
7) When in schedule, the manuscript is copyedited—preferably by whomever hasn't read it yet, but that's not always possible.
8) Copyedited manuscript sent to production department with all pertinent instructions regarding front and back matter, etc.
9) Months later, galleys or repros are returned to the editors.
10) Ideally, whoever did not copyedit the manuscript proofreads the galleys.
11) Galleys returned to the production department for corrections.
12) Corrected galleys sent to the editors. They must be double-checked lest new errors were made while correcting the original mistakes.
13) Corrected galleys returned to production—all okay.
14) Page proofs or repros sent to the editors. These are reproductions of how the body of the book will actually appear, paginated. Last chance for editors to be sure there are no errors, nothing has been omitted and that the page numbers are correct.
15) Page proofs or repros returned to production.
16) Signatures or brownlines sent to the editors to be sure no pages fell out. Too late to change anything short of a disastrous oversight!
17) Signatures back to production department.
18) Editors receive advance copies of the bound book, and send off author's free copies. Usually a month before on-sale date.

Proofreaders' Marks

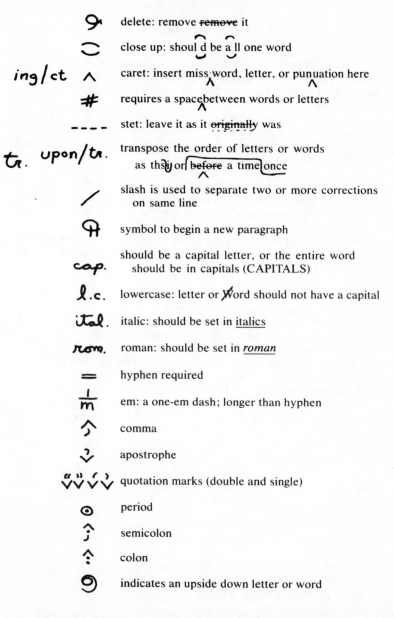

delete: remove ~~remove~~ it

close up: shoul d be a ll one word

caret: insert miss word, letter, or punuation here

requires a space between words or letters

stet: leave it as it ~~originally~~ was

transpose the order of letters or words
as th⌇ or ~~before~~ a time once

slash is used to separate two or more corrections
on same line

symbol to begin a new paragraph

should be a capital letter, or the entire word
should be in capitals (CAPITALS)

lowercase: letter or Word should not have a capital

italic: should be set in italics

roman: should be set in *roman*

hyphen required

em: a one-em dash; longer than hyphen

comma

apostrophe

quotation marks (double and single)

period

semicolon

colon

indicates an upside down letter or word

Details, Details . . .

Understanding your contract—or even a portion of it—takes some explanation. Of course, if you have a good agent, you won't have to know any of this . . . but what if she or he isn't a good agent? Better you should know.

I'm not going to cover every single detail that most paperback contracts contain; that would be a book unto itself. Moreover, contracts vary from publisher to publisher; it all depends on whose lawyer is trying to confuse you more.

Grant of rights or territory.   This says where the publisher may sell your novel in the English language. Generally, paperback companies want the right to sell your romance in any English-speaking country in the world.

Delivery of manuscript.   This is usually quite easy to understand; if the contract says "typescript," that's the same thing as manuscript—more frequently used in England than here.

Revisions.   If the contract you receive doesn't cover this subject, you might want to request that it be added to your contract. In essence, you are agreeing to any ordinary changes in your manuscript, consistent with reasonable standards of publication. This will also include your agreement to a change of title.

If you are dealing with an established, reputable company, you really have nothing to fear. Silhouette, for instance, is a division of Pocket Books, which in turn is owned by Simon & Schuster. However, with the unprecedented success of romances, there are bound to be some entrepreneurs getting into the act sheerly for profits (they have no love for books, couldn't care less about the authors, etc.). Some of them are well intentioned but ignorant of the business; some just plain don't give a damn about anything other than profits.

Should you find yourself dealing with an "unknown quantity," you may want to ask for a more specific Revisions clause. Try to get a clause that limits and specifies the extent of any revisions of your work. Something like: Author agrees to grant Publisher the right to correct all typographical and grammatical errors within the Work; any other revision or changes in the original Work shall be subject to Author's written approval.

Now, you might not win that point. And again, reputable, established publishers *never* substantially change a writer's book without discussing it first. I am only concerned with some of the fly-by-nights whose integrity hasn't been proven. I once had a novel accepted for publication and it was published while I was out of the country. When I saw the printed book, I nearly broke down and wept. Some editor had *added* five and a half pages of totally needless, tasteless sex, and completely changed the ending of my book from upbeat to a downer. It was too late; there was nothing I could do. Why didn't I sue? I tried. I called the best publishing lawyer in the USA, and while he was sympathetic, he made it very clear that it would be impossible to *prove* that my work had been altered. A carbon copy isn't "proof"; I could have typed a different one for myself.

If you don't already know that Circle Of Love is a division of Bantam Books, or that Love & Life is a division of Ballantine (which is owned by Random House), try to figure out a polite, discreet way to inquire just who you're dealing with. It won't be easy, and you certainly don't want to risk besmirching a perfectly innocent company's reputation . . . but do your best.

I could suggest that you ask: "By the way, are you an independent romance publisher, or a division of one of the big companies?" However, now that the question is incorporated into this book, every editor will know where you got the idea in the first place and at least one eye will narrow suspiciously.

Author's alterations. Pretty clear, and for the most part, already covered in this book.

Guaranty and royalties. This is probably one of the most commonly misunderstood clauses. "Guaranty" can also be termed "Advance Against Royalties," and is more commonly used than "Guaranty."

An Advance Against Royalties is a loan from the publisher to you. In category fiction, there is generally a ceiling on what an editor can offer you; however, at some firms, it can range from a low of $2,000.00 to a high of $10,000.00. (We are not speaking about writers with proved records at this point.) The advance is based on how well the editor and publisher think your novel will sell.

It is not repayable. Even if only one copy of your book sold—to your mother, for instance—you still do not have to repay that money. (Should a contract state that you do, watch out!) It is a "loan," however, to the extent that it is later *deducted* from how much your romance earns in royalties after publication. So when you read about Big Name authors getting hundreds of thousands of dollars as an advance, think about two things: (1) It means that author will not see another dime until the book has earned that much money; and (2) it means that author will have to pay taxes on a big chunk of money instead of spreading out the income over the years. (Some famous writers do, by the way, have clauses added wherein the publisher is restrained to smaller payments, no matter how much is really due to the author. I think this is foolhardy. Why should I let the publisher make money on my money? If I become rich and famous, I'm sure I could come up with a few tax shelters of my own, thank you.)

All right, the term is "Advance Against Royalties." What are royalties? They are a *percentage* of the *retail price* of your book, and most publishers have a change in royalty after a certain number of copies of the book have been sold. (Do not confuse how many books are printed with actual sales figures.) You'll hear agents and editors talk about "she got four and six, breaking at 150 thou." Translation: The author receives four percent of the retail price of the book, for the first 150,000 copies sold; she will receive six percent of the retail price for all copies sold after that. Take heed—we are talking about the number of copies *sold,* not how many were printed. It's a distinction too many writers fail to grasp; a publisher may bring out 500,000 copies of your book, but that does *not* mean that all 500,000 will be sold.

Some paperback companies offer six and eight percent, breaking either at 100,000 or 150,000 copies sold. Some very lucky authors (and only if the editor is burning to buy that manuscript!) might even get eight and ten percent. Some companies offer a sliding scale of four, six, eight, and ten, breaking at every x-number of copies sold.

This is among the areas where contracts can be negotiated. Obviously, you have to have a good track record before any editor will discuss such matters; or a good agent. For the sake of conversation, let's pretend you've had three romances published previously, and each of them sold better than 300,000 copies. You're dissatisfied with the treatment you've received from your former publisher and want to go elsewhere with your newest romance.

Your agent has sent the new one to Publisher Z, who can only offer you $10,000.00 as an advance. Okay, it's just a loan anyhow. But: As a concession for letting your new book go "so cheaply," your agent pushes for higher royalty rates, and preferably, breaking at smaller increments. That doesn't mean the publisher will concede to everything your agent asks for, but because of your popularity, there is room for negotiation.

Let's say that your first contract specifies four and six percent, breaking at 150,000 copies sold. Until you know what the retail price is going to be, that doesn't tell you very much. It is permissible to ask your editor what the retail price of your book will be; as a category book, the cover prices are generally within a fixed range. You're told that the retail price will be $2.25. What does this mean to you in dollars and cents?

4% of $2.25 = .09¢ per copy sold
6% of $2.25 = .135¢ per copy sold
150,000 copies sold @ .09¢ each = $13,500.00

Subtract from that how much you were paid as an advance and you'll know how much you can earn in royalties for the first 150,000 copies sold (not printed, but *sold*). For every copy sold beyond that initial 150,000 copies, you will receive .135¢ in royalties.

A word of caution is necessary, much as I hate to rain on anyone's parade. Few first novels ever earn more than the advance paid. Romances frequently fare better because they are so very popular. All I'm suggesting is that you act with prudence. If you run out and open up a bunch of charge accounts, or overextend yourself on what "can" happen, you could be in a peck of trouble. Wait till you've got your royalty check in your bank before you spend a dime of it—*please!*

You should also be aware of the fact that paperback publishers always withhold a certain amount from your royalty checks against "returns." As discussed on page 64, paperback books are sold on consignment; retailers return for credit any unsold books (or their covers).

This is a very touchy area with retailers, distributors, and publishers alike. The book is printed and bound, shipped to the distributor (along with the other books for that month), and the distributor sees to it that the number of copies ordered by each retailer is delivered. However, that retailer is also receiving that month's shipments from numerous other paperback houses, magazine publishers, and so on. It is not rare for a carton of books to be "temporarily" placed out of the way . . . and never, ever opened to be put on sale. A few months down the road, and somebody suddenly discovers this unopened carton. It's too late to put the book on sale, so it goes back to the distributor or publisher for credit.

Even if this doesn't happen (and it is quite seldom), the publisher has no way of predicting just how well your book is selling. Until *all* retailers have sent back the "returns," the basis of computing what is due you in royalties is nothing more than an educated guess.

It is traditional in paperback publishing to withhold as much as twenty percent (fifteen percent is fairer) from your royalty check against unforeseeable "returns." I would like to see the percentage specified as part of the contract, but few publishers agree to that. Nowadays, with sales lagging, there is an increasing swing to holding back more and more against "returns." There's little we can do about it.

If the publisher has more than one division, your contract may include what the royalty rate will be should your manuscript be published under a different imprint; this isn't very likely, but it looks impressive.

And there's usually a different royalty rate for any copies of your book that are sold as premiums. This could be a bulk sale of the book as, say, a giveaway for a new perfume, or bulk sale to your local bank as a public relations gesture, and so forth.

Subsidiary rights. In show business, this is called ancillary rights. Same soup, different noodles. This is only a division between you and publisher of all profits made from any source *other* than the sale of your romance: book club, movies, TV, magazine serialization and so forth and so on. As popular as romances are, I fail to understand why it is publishers (or some clever independent soul) aren't offering tee-shirts with pictures of the better-selling authors. That would also come under Subsidiary Rights as a merchandising sale.

Most paperback companies like to get a fifty-fifty split on all such earnings. The Authors Guild is fighting it, and good agents snicker derisively at such futile hopes. However, since this is your very first sale, don't be offended. Again, with so many romances rubbing elbows in the racks, the prospects for you to make any big monies as a result of a Subsidiary Rights sale are quite slim. In fact, you've got two chances: slim and none. That's not to say that it *can't* happen; it's simply highly unlikely. After decades of writing romances, all of them huge successes, only one flick has been made from Barbara Cartland's prolific output— and at that, it was made for TV, not as a feature film. Since she's still the "queen" of romances, figure the odds for your own first, second (etc.) novel. Not very good.

And as I have told writers for so many years, it's better to have fifty percent of something than one hundred percent of zero. Especially if you're unagented. If the publisher knows it will see half of all monies from such sales, it's an incentive to try to peddle Subsidiary Rights. If the publisher gets no percentage, it becomes a matter of yawning indifference.

The Authors Guild stance is that publishers should only make profits from the business they're in: Publishing. That any monies earned from other sources should go entirely to the author. In principle, I agree with the Guild. In practical reality, a sale is a sale is a sale. You can't drive home a deal like that until you're a name author; and you can't become a name author until you've been published. It's not too different from you can't get a job without experience, but no one will give you a job so you can gain the experience. If a publisher offers you a contract for your first manuscript—grab it!

Copyright. This clause is almost always clear-cut and easy to understand. The publisher will file for copyright at its own expense (a modest sum). Most publishers will automatically put the copyright in your name. I don't know of a single major, important publishing company that would dream of demanding the copyright be in the company name—unless, perhaps, it's a special work they hired someone to write.

Termination. More frequently called "Reversion of Rights." If the contract sent to you doesn't have such a clause, ask that it be included as a rider to the contract. Few will withhold this clause from you, if any. But it's a vitally important part of your contract.

Your book is published in May, right? It sells rather well and then sales taper off and cease altogether. It will definitely be at the retail level for a month; longer than that becomes problematical. If you hang around any store that sells paperbacks, you'll notice that only the Big Name authors, or topical books, remain on sale beyond a month or so. (Unless it's a very small store that doesn't bother to return books, preferring to sell out the stock with slow, occasional sales of the title.)

There are valid reasons for this. Paperbacks are distributed in the basic manner of magazines and periodicals. You don't see last week's or month's issues on sale once that week or month has passed, right? The same is true with paperbacks. "Hey, wait a minute! Romances aren't magazines, and they're not dated material!" Right. I didn't say you'd be happy with the information, did I? That's the way they're distributed and sold. Period.

There are more than 40,000 new books published every year in this country; and there are fewer than 2,000 "official" book stores; this is increasing somewhat with the advent of shopping malls. The quotes because I'm discounting drug stores, or supermarkets, which also carry paperbacks, but aren't in the primary business of selling books. A print run of less than 30,000 copies of a single title means (in paperback terms) that the book probably shouldn't have been published in the first place. It has nothing to do with the quality of writing, but with the ability of the publisher to saturate the marketplace. Paperback lead titles can have print runs of 100,000 copies, or even a million copies. If you multiply the minimum print run of 30,000 times at least 40,000 new books . . . you begin to see that availability of retail space is a very serious problem to paperback companies. Retailers want to stock books that will move off their shelves or racks in a hurry; they must make room for the *next* month's shipment of books to them.

Remember, most hardcover houses go by seasons and there is no set number of books they must publish at any given time. Paperback houses *must* publish x-number of titles every single month, month in and month out. It's a very different kind of business! What didn't sell at the retail level last month will be shipped back to the publisher even as the company is sending out the current month's list of books. The new books have to be put *some*where if the retailer is going to make any money. As a publisher, what would you choose to do: Push the new books that stand a chance to sell quickly; or try to find new outlets for a book that has already had its crack at the market and didn't do too well? Obviously, you'd push the new books.

All right, let's pick it up at the beginning. Your book has been published and was on sale for a month. Weeks go by, then months, then years—your novel is totally forgotten by the publishing company. The corporate attitude (though not your editor's) toward you is pretty much the same as Casanova's feelings toward last week's fling. "It's over; don't embarrass us both with pleading."

If you do not have a Reversion of Rights clause, you are really unable to do anything more about your novel. With a Reversion of Rights clause, however, it's like getting a divorce. You may not still be a virgin, but at least you're free to wed again.

The novel has been off sale (not available at any retail store), and perhaps even considered out of print (no longer available anywhere) by your publisher. With a Reversion of Rights clause, you send a written request for all rights to your novel to be reverted to you within x-number of days (usually anywhere from thirty days to six months), *or* that the publisher must republish your book, generally within six months to a year as of your written notification/request.

Probably, the publisher will revert the rights to you—unless, in the interim, you've had yet another novel published that has done quite well.

With that reversion (and be sure you get it in writing, not just a verbal "Oh, sure"), you are then free to sell your book to some other publisher in the USA. However, let's be practical about this. Almost no paperback publisher is going to want your novel; it's been in paperback before, and those readers who wanted it have already bought it. No hardcover house will be interested because it's already been in paperback (maximum exposure has taken place).

So why is it so important to get the rights back? Because you can wait a few years and sell it to a smaller company; you'll get peanuts, but at least the book's on sale again. Or, as mentioned before, you may come up with a bestselling novel . . . at which point, anything you've ever written might well be of interest to a publisher. This is a crazy business, and almost anything can happen. Play if safe. Get the rights back.

First refusal or option.   This clause is standard publishing procedure. If you ask that it be struck from the contract, a goodly number of publishers will agree to do so. If they won't, then you can ask for more specific terminology in the clause.

The thinking behind the First Refusal or Option clause is that the publisher takes a chance when buying your book, and spends a considerable amount of money to get it out to the retailers. Maybe your first book does just so-so. In order to recoup on the investment, the publisher would like to have the right to consider your next book for publication. That sounds straightforward and reasonable.

However, do not forget just how busy Edna Editor is. So you send her your next manuscript, and it takes her six months to get around to reading it. Maybe she buys it, and maybe she hates it. You've just lost six months by fulfilling your Option clause terms . . . six months in which the manuscript might have already sold to someone else, or have been to three publishers. This clause can cost you a lot of time, and possible income.

Or, let's say that you adored working with Edna, but she has since moved on to another company. You hate the new editor—you are stuck with the new one because of the Option clause.

Or, you decide to write a new book that isn't a romance, but a serious how-to book on making your own stained-glass windows. It's obviously not for Raging Romances, but you have to submit it anyhow because of the Option clause. Again, lost time and possible income.

So how do you avoid these pitfalls? If you can't get the clause struck from the contract, ask that it be reworded. (1) That the option apply only to your *next* manuscript in the *same* category. Your book on stained glass wouldn't have to be submitted to Raging Romances at all. (2) That the company *must* make its decision about your new book within thirty days of its receipt. While that makes it tough on Edna, still it's only fair that your work not be tied up for months and months.

I know several writers who have had their new manuscripts tied up with their publishers (not all the same company) for as much as a year because the Option clause was too vague. And push come to shove, there's an old trick to worm your way out of an Option clause even though you agreed to it in the contract. Spend a few days writing thirty to fifty pages of an abominable, unpublishable manuscript, and send it in. The moment it's rejected, you're quit of any responsibility. Ancient MacManus proverb: Play fair with me, and I shall play fair with you.

Delay of performance.   This clause (it may have a different name from company to company) is pretty standard with most publishing firms. If it isn't in your contract, ask that it be incorporated as a rider.

What it does is assure you that if the publisher should fail to publish your work within a given period (frequently eighteen months to two years), it forfeits all rights to the work, and you are released from your contract. Most contracts will limit this "failure" to any reason *other* than those beyond their control: war, Act of God, fire, flood, etc.

The chances of an established publisher failing to publish your work are next to nil. However, if you are selling your novel to a small, new company, it's wise to be sure this clause is included. Publishing books costs a very large amount of money, and you'll want to protect yourself in case the small company runs out of funds before your manuscript reaches the book-buying public.

As long as we're talking about the dull side of being a romance writer, a few words about income taxes. Save all your receipts from stationery stores for paper, typewriter ribbons, pencils, or *anything* else you buy related to writing your romance. Save all maintenance or repair slips for your typewriter, too. Books that you buy for reference, the cost of film and developing for any snapshots you take with regard to locale for your novel—any expense (inclusive of buying your editor a drink, if she permits you to) related to your book is a bona fide tax deduction, *if* you sell your novel.

Because this is your first book, the IRS and state tax laws will not allow you to make any such deductions unless you have sold your work. Once you've made that sale—even if it's on December 31st—you are then a "professional" writer. A percentage of your rent or mortgage can be deducted; so can a percentage of your utilities, telephone, and any business-related entertaining. As a professional writer, you are self-employed and must file your income tax returns with that status clearly understood. Agent's commissions, postage, paying someone to type your manuscript neatly, the cost of making Xerox copies of your work, depreciating that new typewriter you might have to buy . . . if they pertain to the writing of your romance, which has been contracted for by a publisher, they are legitimate tax deductions as a self-employed individual.

And if you don't live in New York City or Boston, you may find yourself having to explain more to your accountant than the accountant can tell you. However, don't plague your tax accountant until you've got a contract; why add to his or her burden until you know that the information will be required?

Most of the other standard contractual clauses are quite easy to understand. There may be lots of legalese about remaindering your book, no royalties on copies published in Braille, etc., but don't worry about them. The important thing is to get that first contract.

I certainly would not refuse a contract for my first novel because I didn't get my way with any of these clauses. I mention them only so you'll know what's involved. There's no harm in asking your editor if this or that might be changed (with a lilting tone and a smile in your voice!) . . . but be prepared for the answer to be "No." There's very little latitude with romances; especially for beginning writers.

Fanfare and Hoopla

I know, I know . . . you've read in the paper how much Pocket Books spent on promoting Janet Dailey's last novel, or that she was on Donahue's show; and you've read about Barbara Cartland's national tour, and so forth. Why, John Jakes has made well over a million dollars in royalties with his Kent Family Chronicles (which was only half the total sum of royalties, since the creator of the saga, Lyle Kenyon Engel, received the other half). "Goodness gracious, Miss Scarlett, there's a fortune to be made out there! Why isn't my publisher promoting my book?"

The truth is a matter of sheer economics.

Paperback publishers have what is known as lead titles. (Lead, as in leading someone by the nose; not lead, as what's used to make pencils—English is a silly language.) Every month, there's a meeting of the key personnel to decide which will be the #1, #2, or #3 title for an upcoming list of books. Who among the staff are present will vary from company to company. I've worked at companies where just about anyone could sit in on these meetings; and at others, where it was so closed-door that the editors were the last to learn of the decisions made. So let's go back to Raging Romances and set up a hypothetical situation.

Edna Editor and her associate will definitely be in attendance; they're the only two who have read the books scheduled for publication. Their boss will be there, too; probably a V.P. and editorial director. The publicity director, and the head of sales, plus whoever is in charge of subsidiary rights. This meeting takes place well before any salesmen go out into the field to solicit advance orders; and in all probability, even before the cover has been decided on.

The meeting is to choose which of Edna's four books in that month will get whatever advertising budget Raging Romances is either willing to spend, or can afford to. It is also to decide (1) how much to spend on cover artwork, and (2) how large a first printing the book should have.

As you can readily see, these decisions are all rooted in money: How much to spend for what.

Edna really thinks your first novel, *Romance Of My Own,* is fabulous. It's fresh, free from clichés, moves smoothly, has a solid plot that hasn't been worked to death and a very unusual career for the heroine—unusual in romances, not in real life. *Romance Of My Own* has everything going for it; originality, pace, and it's like a breath of fresh air in a world staggering under the weight of hundreds of romances.

Whether Edna has taken a liking to you or not has nothing to do with anything. This is Big Business, not a Wives of the Grange dinner. (No, that's not a put-down of the Grange; it's only that such functions are purely social.) There are a few writers I've met whom I have come to love dearly as real, trusted, and respected friends. However, at a meeting of this kind, such considerations must be put aside. It is the book that counts—not Jim's adorable cleft chin or Marsha's caring support during one of my personal crises. (Sorry, Jim and Marsha—but you know it's true.) It is the editor's responsibility to push the book that stands the very best chance of success in the marketplace.

In some ways, it's not fair (she said, wearing her writer's hat). After all, Harold Robbins doesn't *need* the push for success; his books sell no matter what he writes or what the reviewers might say. Logically

speaking, it's the unknown author who should get the company's advertising budget. It just doesn't work that way as a rule.

The exception is if the new writer is a "find," or has written a
romance too marvelous to pass over. (I would have loved to sit in when
the meeting was taking place to decide how to promote Rosemary
Rogers' first historical romance. . . . I'll bet there was a lot of Gelusil
and Librium consumed till the campaign was proved a success!)

Sadly, all too few first novels are worthy of a big expenditure.
They're "good," or they're "okay," but not outstanding. A one-time
advertisement, one-half page, in *The New York Times'* Book Review
Section costs $5,150. Similarly, a one-time ad, also one-half page, in the
industry's leading publication, *Publishers Weekly,* costs $1,370. In the
paperback industry, profits are measured in pennies per book—not
dollars. The only reason paperback companies can survive is because of
volume sales.

American paperback companies operate on the theory that it is best
to overprint a book to allow for returns, and to reach the maximum
number of retail outlets. English paperback companies take a more
conservative view; they only print what they are confident they can sell.
If the book sells out, they go back to press. It is more expensive to go
back to press than to have a large initial print run. It's a moot point as to
which is the better approach—though I know that the English have next
to no problems with returns; they don't glut the market in the first place.

But let's say that Raging Romances plans an average print run of
75,000 copies (not a lead title, obviously). If they sell sixty percent of
that, they're content; if they sell seventy percent, they are happy; if they
sell eighty percent, they're excited; and if they sell ninety percent,
there's cause for jubilation. Needless to say, any sales beyond that
render editors catatonic from excessive euphoria.

So before any decision can be reached on how much to spend on
advertising, they must decide which book is the most likely to succeed.
Again, first novels rarely do. The reading public is more likely to spend
its money on authors whom it's already read and enjoyed. Publishers
know that.

If Gertie Glutz is already an established seller for Raging Romances,
in all probability her newest book will be targeted for the ad budget—
even though yours is a far better book.

However, Edna is really in there championing your romance. "All
right," she concedes. "Gertie gets the number-one spot for the May list.
Romance Of My Own should be Number Two."

"Wait a sec," says the subsidiary rights director. "Is there something you're not telling me? Is her romance outstanding enough that I
could lay it on magazine editors for excerpting or serialization?"

"Definitely," Edna says, crossing her fingers under the table. *"Romance Of My Own* should do very well with women's magazines . . . not

to mention that it has a very strong dramatic rights potential. In the hands of the right director, it could be another *Love Story,* except with an upbeat ending."

"Really," drawls the publicity director, skeptical. "What about the author. Is she presentable?"

Edna smiles tolerantly but pleasantly. "I haven't met her yet, but I've spoken to her on the phone. She's articulate, charming, and definitely not the sort to kick up her heels in girlish glee."

"Spare me," groans the publicity director, good-naturedly.

There's a round of: "Right," "Yeah," "Boy, you can say that again!"

"I don't know," the editorial director intervenes. "The other two romances for May are from authors we've published previously. Why should we spend anything for this complete unknown?"

Edna shakes her head. "The other two titles are so-so, nothing more. If *Romance Of My Own* doesn't outsell them, I'll eat my blue pencil."

"Very amusing," the editorial director replies, clearly not amused.

Edna glances at her furtively, trying to assess what mood she's in. She already knows that the editorial director is the type who runs hot and cold; she's either behind you one hundred percent, or she's wondering if it isn't time to consider replacing you. One mistake can tip the balance.

"Can I call her a star, another Helen Van Slyke?"

"Sure," Edna responds to the publicity director. "Without exaggeration, too!"

"Well, I'm still not convinced," the editorial director states with deadly calm. "What do you think?" she asks the head of sales, who has a synopsis of the book.

He strokes his chin thoughtfully. "There are a lot of women in the computer technology field—it might be worth a shot."

And so the meeting proceeds. Which book should get the expensive foil on the cover; which gets standard treatment. If they spend the money for a foil cover, or a wraparound cover, or even a die-stamped cutout . . . they're going to have to be pretty sure of recouping the investment. That means a larger print run (the larger the printing, the lower the unit cost of producing the book). And if they go to that expense, they'll almost have to do *some* advertising (your hometown paper, perhaps) in hopes of convincing the public to buy the book. For a while, it looks pretty sure that your romance will be the #2 for May. At the last moment, the editorial director says: "It's too risky."

The head of sales, being a yes-man, says: "You may be right. Why don't we wait to see how this first one does, and then maybe promote her next romance?"

And that's that. You've lost. *Romance Of My Own* will be an also-ran, trailing at the bottom of the list. No advertising budget, no real promotional efforts, less push from the sales force, and subsidiary rights will do what it can—but not assertively. Hard as Edna tried, there's only room for one #1 or #2; there's no #1-a.

Naturally, you don't know that any of this has transpired. You're still regaling everyone at the office, or your neighbors, with what a huge success your novel will be—just you wait and see. April rolls around and you receive the advance copies of your book. All right, so the heroine isn't really a redhead on the cover, but sort of a strawberry blonde; why the hero is shown holding the heroine as if about to break her in half, you don't know—it wasn't in the story at all. The front cover blurb reads: "Her only hope of marriage to Bill shattered in the arms of another man." It did? That wasn't in the book either. Oh, well. You've got the published book in your hands and, if you put on your glasses, you can clearly read your name on the cover. Or maybe those things *were* in your novel; it's been so long since you finished writing it, maybe you forgot. The main thing is that it was published. You can hardly wait for *Romantic Times* to call you for an interview, or for the reviews that will appear in national magazines. And there's still a whole month to go before your romance is even on sale!

Then it's May. Yup. You saw two copies of *Romance Of My Own* on sale at the supermarket. But it's not at the dimestore, or the market on the other side of town. What's going on? You're a famous author—aren't you? Answer: No. And you mustn't personalize. A frantic phone call to Edna will get you nowhere; it's totally out of her hands. (And the more hysterical you get, the less inclined she'll be to buy your next manuscript.)

Why isn't your book on sale everywhere? Any number of reasons might be valid. Maybe that dimestore is notoriously slow to pay its bills; Raging Romances no longer bothers with them at all. They're more trouble than they're worth. Maybe the supermarket on this side of town buys from a different jobber than the one on the other side of town. Maybe the book buyer only had so much space in his racks, so took only two titles from the May list. Maybe a lot of things. It is *not* the "fault" of your publisher; the company needs to make as many sales as possible to stay in business.

You are bitterly disappointed and a whole lot dejected. All your work, your hopes, shot down. Your neighbors look at you pityingly; your husband tries to buoy up your spirits, but to no avail. Friends in Los Angeles or Tulsa write to ask where they can find your romance; it's not on sale in their area. Why did you fill out the publicity questionnaire if no one at Raging Romances was going to use the fact that you belong to several women's clubs or that your spouse is a bigshot with the Knights of Columbus?

The answer is that *Romance Of My Own* wasn't #1 or #2 on Raging

Romances' list for May. To borrow from the popular song: "Is that all there is?" Yes and No.

Try to find out as early as you can what Raging Romances plans for your book. This may be decided at an editorial meeting, a promotion meeting, or even at the sales force meeting. Do this sleuthing shortly after the contract has been executed and returned to you by a friendly letter or phone call to Edna: "At what stage does Raging Romances determine which will be its lead title for the month? When does that take place?"

Armed with that information, make a note to yourself on the calendar to contact Edna again about a week after the meeting will have taken place. Graciously inquire if you were lucky enough to make the #1 or #2 spot with your romance. If yes—smile a lot for the rest of the day and take your husband out to some romantic restaurant for dinner. If no, *all is* not *lost!*

Ask Edna when she expects to receive advance covers, the ones that are issued to the sales force; then request that she send you one (not a hundred—just one). As busy as Edna is, she may well forget to send it to you, but you've noted when they're expected, so drop her a postcard as a gentle reminder. You are going to do your own hype for your romance!

To accomplish this, find out from Edna the correct name and proper title of the person in charge of direct sales; if Raging Romances has an 800 number, find that out, too (many publishers don't, but they will accept collect calls from retailers—verify this).

Okay. You have now received an advance cover of your book. (There's a hole punched in the upper right-hand corner of the cover; this will not appear when your book is bound. The reason for it is to avert anyone using that cover illegally, sending it back to the publisher for a credit.) On the back of the cover, paste a plain sheet of paper with the typewritten information about who's in charge of direct sales, and what number to telephone or where to write.

Take a clipboard and curl up with your telephone directory. You are going to make a list of all the bookstores you can contact; all the other places that sell paperbacks (drugstores, discount stores, etc.) in your area. And, a list of local newspapers, throwaways, regional magazines; and every other possible source for review of your romance, or free publicity. Once you have tallied all these places, march directly to your local quick-print store and run off as many copies of the original cover as you will require. To save money, ask the person to turn the paper over and run it through again, this time with the information about who to contact regarding direct sales.

I used to be extremely shy about tooting my own horn; it was, after all, poor manners to brag or pitch my own work. It's false modesty. You wrote the book; you want it to be on sale, available, and read. More importantly, you want the sales to be impressive—*not* just for the royalties, but to show Raging Romances that you are a profitable author for *them*. If your book doesn't sell very well, why should they consider the purchase of your next one?

Everyone knows that Jackie Susann's *Valley Of The Dolls* was a bestseller, and continues to this day to enjoy very good sales. What few people outside the industry realize is how this came to be. For years, *The New York Times* Book Review Section has carried a list of bestsellers, based on sales reported by selected local retailers. This list of retailers was sacrosanct; a lot more so than which households are hooked up to the Nielson monitor for TV ratings. As it is told in publishing circles, Ms. Susann somehow managed to acquire a list of which stores reported to the *Times*. Then, as soon as her novel was published, she spent a fortune going to each and every one of those retailers, and bought up copies of *Valley Of The Dolls*. Result? The stores reported that they couldn't keep her book in stock, that it was selling like the proverbial hotcakes.

Well, of course, the novel climbed to #1 on the bestseller list in very short order. And Americans being what we are, we all rushed out to buy the latest bestseller . . . which, in turn, really legitimatized the status. One version has it that Ms. Susann bought so many copies of her book that she had to rent a garage to store them. (The *Times,* by the way, has since changed its modus operandi—you couldn't pull that trick today.)

Another example was that of an unknown writer from whom I had bought a mystery. It was probably one of the worst books I ever saw to press. I put it into schedule with gritted teeth, my eyes clamped shut, and a fresh string of worry beads. I simple *had* to have one more title for that month's list, and it was all that was available to me. I could only hope that the cover art, the sell copy, and the category would carry the day— and that I didn't receive dozens of poison-pen letters from irate readers.

Shortly after the mystery was published, I was informed that it was doing very well—was I planning to buy another mystery from this writer? To say I was shocked is to put it mildly. I mean, it was *really* a terrible novel, and I knew we hadn't spent a dime to advertise or promote it. What had happened? Assuming the tone and attitude of ever-the-gracious-editor, I telephoned my author to share the good news with him. In truth, my motive was sheer curiosity; he was not only a poor writer, but also a pain in the neck.

Naturally, he was pleased with the news. He then proceeded to tell me that he had personally hounded book retailers, local newspapers, and so on, about his book. On his own, this writer had turned a probable disaster into a profitable surprise. He'd contacted his old schools and talked them into running reviews of his book for the school papers; since he worked with a major corporation that had its own newsletter, they raved about his mystery. By sheer dogged determination, he saw to it that his book was on sale and reviewed—publisher be damned.

And you can, too. Bear in mind, though, that if Raging Romances *is* going to put some teeth into the promotion of your novel . . . *stay out of it!* Do not step on their publicity director's lines. Render unto Caesar what is Caesar's, and unto publicity what is publicity's. If they're going to do a job for you, the last thing in the world they want from you is intervention or, worse, "double planting."

But if they're not going to give your romance a push, then swing away. Local cable television needs all the material it can get; offer yourself as a guest for interview. If you're too shy to do it, then ask a friend to make the suggestion. Offer to be a guest speaker at the local high school, or if there's a creative writing class at a nearby college, contact the instructor and volunteer your services. Whatever you can think of that might help to sell your book is fair play, provided the publisher has no plans of its own.

If you are among the Chosen, wonderful. Do not expect it to happen with your very first romance; that would be unrealistic. But at least you now know how to promote your own romance—push come to shove.

Do not—as happened not too long ago—rent an airplane and buzz your publisher's offices. I don't really blame the person who did it, mind you. Publishing can be very frustrating; but if he'd read this book first, he could have saved the cost of renting a plane, and avoided the subsequent arrest. Publishers often work in mysterious ways, but they generally do have valid reasons for their actions . . . or lack of action.

The Denouement

As you can see for yourself, you're rapidly reaching the end of this how-to book—are your palms growing moist? Fear not. This book will not self-destruct. If you need to refer back to it frequently, don't be embarrassed about it.

Your characters and the plot are the most important aspects of writing a romance; the story must be vivid, colorful, and flow with ease.

You have read dozens and dozens of romances and already know which kind you enjoy the most. You've written to the publisher and requested its latest set of guidelines; these will change with market needs, so it's pointless to include them all. Most of them will tell you just how far they want you to go with love scenes; some will even help you out by stating what's been overdone within their own lists of romances.

You've blocked out the plot lines for at least six romances of the type you enjoy; and have then sat down with family or friends to work out your own plot, following the examples of the novels you've read. Are the locales exotic or not; is the hero always about ten years older than the heroine; does your heroine have a distinctive career or doesn't it matter; and so forth.

By now, you have learned how to avoid static, dull writing; how important action verbs can be and visual descriptions. And you know how to prepare a manuscript.

You, intrepid reader, are about to embark on a whole new career. You may not earn a great deal of money with your first romance, but as you improve, and your name is seen more frequently at paperback racks, you will earn more and more.

The decision of whether or not to seek an agent has been made simple for you; and you know the editorial process your romance will go through. You also know what to expect when your romance is published.

You are better prepared at this very moment than any beginning writer I have ever met. There are only two things you have left to fear: A double chin, and a thickening waistline. People who sit at desks for a living ultimately develop both. *Exercise* regularly! I don't. My reward is a double chin and a thickening waistline. I wish I'd read this book when I first started out, and I hope that it will answer all your questions. One day, the popularity of romances—as we see it now—will begin to taper off. But from this day forward, you will never have to worry about that. There will be new popular categories of fiction for women (or even more general fiction), and you will have built the writing muscle to be able to tackle any subject of your choice. In essence, when you are accepted by a publisher, you are being paid to do what you enjoy doing. How bad is that?

Good luck to you all, and welcome to the insane world of publishing!

Glossary of Terms

Advance against royalties: Those monies paid to the author of a book prior to the work's publication. It is usually paid half and half; half the total amount upon execution of the contract, and half upon completion of an *acceptable* manuscript; or in some instances, half on publication of the book.

   The kicker here is the waiting period. Don't expect the first half a few days after you've signed the contract. It's after the publisher has signed it, or an authorized executive. If it's summer holiday time, or peak flu season, that can take awhile. Then, once it's signed, it has to be vouchered for payment and sent to accounting.

Allow two to ten weeks after you've signed the contract before expecting your first check.

Ditto the second half. The editor must read the completed novel, with or without revisions, to be sure it doesn't need any additional work. That's what "acceptable" refers to. If everything's okay, then the second payment will be vouchered; again, allow for the accounting department's delays.

Advance orders: The publisher's sales force, armed with covers of that month's books and any other materials they are provided, go out to the retailers in their territory to solicit orders for the books in advance of publication.

Some publishers offer retailers a special price if books are ordered prior to publication (or even to the general public). Most paperback houses do not.

Advertising: Advertising is paid for; publicity and public relations are not. Advertising encompasses ads in newspapers, magazines, television, or other media. Do not expect your first romance to receive the benefit of any advertising; it might, however, be included in an overall ad for the entire month's list. This is not, though, very likely.

Author's alterations (AA's): Any changes you may make in your romance after the book has already been set in type that veer from what appeared on the original manuscript.

Back matter: Any printed material that appears at the end of your romance. This could be ads for forthcoming romances; a listing of romances already available; or even quotes from happy readers of romances from your publisher.

Blurbs: (See Jacket copy.) Technically, blurbs are quotes from well-known people who are willing to "endorse" your romance with a short comment about its merits.

Brownline/blueline: More commonly used with computer typesetting systems. They are, in essence, the same as signatures.

Certificate of registration of trade name: (See Doing business as.)

Cliff-hanger: Any device at the end of a chapter to pique the reader's curiosity so that she or he will want to turn the page and continue reading.

Copyeditor: (See Editors.)

Copyright: Protection under the law, filed at the Library of Congress, that you own all rights to the romance you've written. However, in signing your contract, what you are doing is temporarily (provided your contract has a Reversion of Rights clause) agreeing to give those rights to your publisher in exchange for a sum of money to be applied against royalties.

Cover artwork: Anything that pertains to how the front and back cover of your romance is presented. The size and style of your romance's title and your name; the positioning of both; how it's to be illustrated; the positioning of the publisher's logo, the book number, its retail price and where the front cover blurb goes, plus any information that goes on the spine.

Wraparound cover: Where the illustration is carried over so if the book is placed facedown and opened, the illustration is continuous from back cover to spine to front cover.

Foil cover: A process whereby the title or other aspects of the cover are done in "shimmering" foil to catch the buyer's eye; ideally, away from other books on display to focus on yours.

Die-stamped cut-out cover: Where a portion of the front cover is mechanically cut out to reveal another illustration beneath.

Cover information: The typewritten information supplied by the editors to the art department. This will include the book's ISBN, retail price, month of publication, title, author, category, front and back cover blurbs, synopsis of the story; and suggested concepts for illustration, inclusive of descriptions of the main characters, and significant dramatic moments from the story itself that lend themselves to illustration.

Delay of performance: A contractual clause wherein the publisher agrees to publish your romance within a specified time, unless prohibited from doing so by extreme outside influence such as war, strikes, Acts of God, and so on.

Direct sales: Any sale of your romance that is not through the publisher's regular distributor or jobber. It may be a book retailer who prefers to deal directly with the publisher; an individual who is having difficulty finding your romance on sale locally; or a women's group wanting to buy a quantity of your romance and is seeking a discount.

Doing business as (d/b/a): A notification to the general public via your town clerk or local newspaper—usually a neighborhood paper—that states you intend to do business under a name different from your own. This enables you to legally sign all documents and contracts under the name you have chosen to conduct business in. Also known as: Certificate of Registration of Trade Name.

Double planting: Most often heard among publicists and public relations personnel. If the publicist at your publishing company sends out a release about your romance to a magazine or reviewer, and you have also contacted the same people, it's known as "double planting." It makes everyone very angry and upset, and is to be avoided.

Editors: Titles will vary depending on the size of the company, and peculiarities of top management (I have worked at companies where there is no editor-in-chief because the owners of the firm didn't want anyone to have such a lofty title). The pecking order is usually as follows:

Executive editor or Editorial director: No one knows for sure which title is higher up than the other unless one works for that particular company. If it's important for you to know, ask.

Editor-in-Chief: Generally, the buck stops with this person; especially if there is no executive editor or editorial director. The ed-in-chf (a little abbreviation humor in the industry) is responsible for the total work flow, often for the future editorial direction of the company, and not only for the quality of the books published by the firm, but also that they are profitable. In some companies, the ed-in-chf is more of an administrator than an editor; at other companies, you'll see the light on in this individual's office long after everyone else has toddled off for a relaxing martini at the end of the day.

Acquisitions editor: Some publishers woo them; others couldn't care less. An acquisitions editor is a publishing talent scout. Usually she or he has a strong rapport with agents, and has been around long enough to have a list of writers who are willing to switch alliances to wherever the acquisitions editor is working at the time. That, or someone who has such persuasive selling powers that she or he can entice better writers away from their current publishers.

Senior editor: There is usually more than one senior editor. It does not have anything (necessarily) to do with longevity with the company so much as on-the-job expertise.

Editor: This can mean anything, depending on which company is involved. If there is only one editor (and none of the above), then that person is the top banana. If, though, there are people at the firm with the above-mentioned titles, then the editor (in all probability) can do the job of the senior editor, but simply hasn't received the promotion as yet.

Associate editor: Might be interchangeable with editor, or someone who is very capable, but not quite ready to fully accept the responsibility of seeing a book through all its stages.

Managing editor: More often than not, the managing editor is responsible for the other editors meeting their deadlines, a smooth flow between editors and the production department, and overseeing that schedules are adhered to. In some companies, however, the managing editor also edits, and is ranked directly beneath the editor-in-chief.

Copyeditor: The person responsible for catching and correcting all your misspellings, typographical errors, incorrect grammar, or unclear sentence structure. This person will also bring to the attention of the editor any questionable areas of your romance such as your writing that it was a Georgian home on page 10, then referring to it as a raised ranch later on; or jarring information such as your stating that the heroine paid $25,000.00 for a VW Beetle. The copyeditor can question the arrangement of your material, or even the content, but is not authorized to make any editorial changes without consulting the editor.

Assistant editor: Higher up than a secretary, but still quite new to the business of editing. Doubtlessly quite young, and forced to live at home due to imposed poverty level via low salary.

Ellipsis(es): The formation of three consecutive dots, or periods, to indicate that one or more words have been deleted from the original material; or to indicate hesitancy or a suspended thought in dialogue or narrative.

Excerpting: The sale to a magazine or periodical of the right to publish a single chapter or portions of your book.

First-person narrative: Books or stories (fiction and nonfiction) told with the viewpoint of "I."

First refusal: (See Option.)

Foil cover: (See Cover artwork.)

Frontispiece: Originally and correctly, this is the illustration that appears before the book actually begins; traditionally, facing the title page. It could be an illustration from the book itself, or a picture of the author. However, it was borrowed into paperback language to refer to a short version of a scene from the book (in fiction) to hook a buyer's interest. It can also be used to describe how important (or funny or whathaveyou) the book is, or to list quotes of the reviews the book has received.

Front matter: All that goes before the body of the book itself (known as "text"). It will include: Frontispiece; a list of other books you've written; the title page; the copyright page; dedication; and possibly a preface or foreword. It can also include a half-title page. Anything prior to the preface or foreword is not paginated; hence, many books begin on page five. If there is a preface or foreword, those pages are numbered in lower-case roman numerals; in which case, your romance might not begin until page 7 or 10, etc.

Galleys: Long, narrow strips of cheap paper on which the body of your book is printed. They are the first stage of physically reproducing your book. The typeset material is as wide as it will be in the bound book, but there is no pagination; just line after line of what has been set into type from your manuscript.

Grant of rights: (See Territory.)

Guaranty: (See Advance against royalties.)

Half title: Seldom seen in paperbacks, but it is a page that has nothing more on it than the title of your romance; your name will not appear, nor the name of the publishing firm. If used at all in mass-market publishing, it's generally because the manuscript ran too short of words and the publisher can't think of any other way to use up an extra two blank pages.

Impulse buyer: Those people who leave their homes to do anything other than buy a book . . . yet end up buying one on the spur of the moment. Illustrators of book jackets are very fond of taking the lion's share of the credit for impulse-buyer sales—they may well be right.

ISBN: Abbreviation for International Standard Book Number. Due to the overwhelming number of books published, or imported, and with the advent of computer technology, retailers, librarians and schools can track down any given title by its ISBN far more quickly than with the old system. In this way, every publisher is assigned an ISBN prefix that no one else in the world has, or can use. It's like, in a way, a Social Security number; only one publisher can have that prefix. After the prefix, the publisher can use any additional numbering system it may choose; but to the computer, only the ISBN counts.

Italics: Represented on your typewriter by underscoring the word or number you select; the printer will know to automatically set any underscored word in italics—letters, numbers, or words that slant to the right.

Jacket copy: "Soon to be a major motion picture," or "Six months on the bestseller lists," or quotes from reviews, or one or more lines to capture the flavor of the book to convince the browser to buy it. Whatever appears on the front or back cover that is written to sell your book is jacket copy, despite the fact that paperbacks do not have jackets. (This, too, was borrowed from hardcover terminology. However, hardcover books seldom have any sell copy on the front cover; instead, it appears on the flyleaf.)

Lead title: Generally, both in hardcover and paperback, one book is selected out of the entire season's or month's list of books to really receive the biggest push with advertising, promotion and so on. It is referred to as the lead title. There may be lesser ones, and they will receive proportionately less of the budget.

Log in: A running register of manuscripts received (as well as hardcover books for reprint possibilities, or works from other nations for publication in this country in paperback format). Date of receipt, author's name and title are shown; if agented, this is often included.

Lower case: Not capitalized.

Mechanical: A pasteup of the cover; front, back and spine, precisely as it is to be printed, except in black and white. The illustration has been scaled to size and positioned perfectly. Overlays of tissues will give all the necessary instructions as to which colors are to appear, where, and a color transparency has been made of the artist's illustration for use by the printer. Some editors (very few) will send trusted authors a Xerox copy of the mechanical so they can get an idea of what their books will look like. Too often, authors—especially novices—panic and want changes, demand different blurbs or another illo (short for illustration). It is best not to send copies 'of the mechanical unless the editor knows the author very, very well.

Merchandising: This encompasses any variety of things from selling your romance as a premium or giveaway by a manufacturer, to arm bands with the title of your book and your name, to figurines being made based on your characters. (Remember *Love Story* and the dolls, plates, and dozens of other non-book products? That's merchandising.) It is the process of capitalizing/profiting on "spin-off" merchandise, gleaned from your book, but not the book itself.

Multiple viewpoint. A novel told from the point of view of two or more characters. A one-line break is required to indicate that we are switching from one character's viewpoint to another's. With each change of viewpoint, it is treated as if it were a first- or third-person narrative; each character can only know what she or he witnesses, is told and so on.

Off sale: When the book has been published and distributed, but is no longer available at the retail level. Usually, some copies would still be available from the publisher directly.

Omniscient viewpoint: The actual definition for omniscient is "having infinite awareness, understanding, and insight; possessed of universal or complete knowledge." It is the form of writing wherein the author knows everything, and reveals it to the reader through several main characters, or by projecting the author's perspective into the book. The characters cannot know anything beyond the rules already explained, but the author may interject knowledge beyond what the characters know. A very tricky viewpoint to handle, best left to highly experienced, professional writers (who are, one expects, fearless).

On sale: The book has been published, distributed, and is currently available at the retail level.

One-line break: A lineal space between paragraphs, in the same chapter, that denotes a change of viewpoint; or, more likely in romances, to alert the reader that we are jumping ahead in time, flashing back, changing locale without a transition, or in any other way indicates a "break" in the sequence of events that precede it.

Option: A clause in a contract that gives the publisher the exclusive right to be the very first company to consider your next book for publication (unless otherwise modified). Also known as First refusal.

Out of print: When a book has been published, distributed, was on sale, then went through a period of off sale. There are no more copies in stock, and there are no plans to go back to press with the book. The contract may still be in force and binding, but your romance is moribund.

Over the transom: A publishing phrase to indicate that a manuscript was submitted without benefit of a query letter or any other form of advance notification to the editor.

Page proofs: The stage following corrected galleys. At this point, the typeset lines have been measured off so they are even at top and bottom, and the pages are numbered. Called repros in computer typesetting.

Paginate: The act of numbering the pages, either of a manuscript or the typeset book.

Partial manuscript: A work in progress, incomplete. Should consist of the opening three chapters, minimum.

Printer: The individual, or company, that literally prints your romance. Typesetting and binding might be done by the printer, or independent companies that specialize in either.

Printing: It is used in one of two ways: Either to indicate how many times your romance has gone to press ("It's had five printings"); or occasionally used to specify how many copies of your book were published ("It had a 300,000-copy first printing").

Print run: More frequently used exclusively for how many copies were printed at one time ("It had an initial print run of 300,000 copies").

Production: The central control of all the mechanical processes involved between turning over the copyedited manuscript to the bound book, ready for shipment to the distributor.

Proofreader: The person(s) who reads the galleys or proofs of your romance immediately following the manuscript being set into type. (Proofreaders' marks on page 69.)

Promotion: The act of giving your book added sales boosts with, for instance, special displays, banners, posters that retailers may place on their windows or inside the store, etc. It can also refer to retailer incentives such as one book free if ten are ordered, or even a prize of a free vacation to the Bahamas.

Public domain: When a work is no longer protected by copyright, either because the term of copyright has expired, or some legality has been trespassed upon. A case in point (older readers might recall) was the publication of the novel *Candy* in the early 1960s. The authors were Americans living in France; the novel was published by a French publisher, but in English. The work was not simultaneously copyrighted in the USA, and according to the laws at that time, this was a violation of copyright protection. While *Candy* was well on its way to becoming a bestseller in this country, several somewhat less than integrity-filled publishers took advantage of this violation, and there were three or four different editions of the same novel on sale concurrently—with no royalties paid to the authors, and no recourse.

Publicity: The generating and disseminating of "news" about your romance. It could be (Oh happy day!) an unexpected snapshot of the First Lady reading your novel on an airplane—which the publicist would instantly have reproduced and sent to every newspaper, TV network and magazine—or a "plant" in *The National Enquirer* that your life would be complete if only you could have a date with Robert Redford. Anything that a publicist can do to promote you and your novel, that obtains media attention, is publicity . . . and it's free.

Publisher: You will soon learn, after your romance is contracted for or published, that few people can tell the difference between a publisher and a printer. A printer is a tradesperson (often an artiste, but still . . .); he or she might also be publishers. A publisher, however, is a person, or persons, or a corporate entity that underwrites all the expenses for the publication of books, and attendant costs such as advertising, overhead, and so forth. A publisher and the salaried or free-lance staff, are responsible for the acquisition of books, readying them for press, and seeing them through to bound books ready for retail sale. The publisher is the top executive (unless you start to get into chairpersons of the board, and all that).

Reader: Larger companies employ readers. These are usually young people anxious to become a part of the publishing industry. The sole responsibility of a reader is to read the manuscripts that are submitted, then type up a book report—with a recommendation for acceptance or rejection. Your romance may have one or two or three readings before it is sent up to a higher editorial authority for final decision.

Reader identification: As the term implies, the ability of whoever is reading your romance to "identify" with the heroine or other main characters. Even though the reader may be a brawny male, as author you should be able to make him understand, and empathize, with your characters—male and female, young or old, etc. Charles Dickens was a master of reader identification; even when his characters were hateful, we still had sympathy for them because we could put ourselves in those characters' places. He made us transcend our own selves and "be" his characters.

Release: A printed page with special information (or an update) about you or your book that is sent to the media in hopes they will want to use it.

Repros: (See Galleys.)

Retail price: The price on the cover of a book.

Returns: Any unsold copies that the retailer returns to the distributor, jobber, or the publisher, for credit.

Reversion of rights: A contractual clause that grants the author the opportunity to reacquire all rights to her or his book, contingent upon the book being no longer in print, and subject to written demand ("demand" shouldn't be taken literally—a cordial request will do).

Roman type: Straight type, not italic—what you're reading now.

Royalties: A percentage of the cover price of a book, payable to the author based on copies sold—not copies printed. The book is generally required to be on sale for at least six months before a royalty report is due. However, depending upon when the book is contracted for, and actually published, this can far exceed six months. A novel might be contracted for in May of this year, yet not be published until July of the following year. It will not have been on sale for a full six months when the next royalty report would be sent to other authors (usually semiannually); consequently, though a July book, no royalty report, or any monies, will be sent until May of the following year. This is not uncommon at all.

Royalty report: Incomprehensible to anyone other than that touted breed known as "any child can do it." Even CPA's don't understand them; I doubt that the royalty departments understand them. They should tell you how many books were printed, how many were distributed and how many are (tentatively) sold—tentatively only because not all the returns are in. Based on your royalty rate, it should say how much you are due, and how much they are withholding against returns. If you can figure out a royalty report, please explain it to me at your earliest opportunity.

Running heads: You've seen them a hundred times and simply didn't know what they were called. It's the line of type at the top of the page, on either left- or right-hand (or both), that carries the name of your book, or your name, or the title of the chapter—or all of it. Seldom done in mass-market paperbacks unless the manuscript runs short and the publisher needs to pad it out by taking up extra space at the top of the pages.

Secondary retail outlets: What it sounds like—not the really big bookstores, or chain bookstores. That is not a slur on the smaller stores; only an indication that they do not buy in sufficient volume to warrant the added shipping expense, warehousing, invoicing, and (sadly) too frequently, delays in paying for the books received. There is a running argument about the plight of small, independently owned bookstores . . . but it would take too much space to cover in this book. Both sides have a valid case.

Sell copy: A catchall term for just about anything that is designed to convince others to buy—whether your efforts to give the editor a sales pitch, promotional materials, or jacket copy.

Serialization: Sometimes a condensed (though usually not) version of the entire book run in consecutive issues of magazines or newspapers.

Signature: A single sheet of paper that, when folded, provides thirty-two pages of consecutive, typeset pages; the last stage prior to going to press for the printing and binding of the book.

Slushpile: The stacks and stacks of manuscripts and partial manuscripts awaiting a first reading.

Style: The decisions required regarding the appearance and format of the body (or text) of the romance.

Subsidiary rights: The sale to others to in some manner use your romance for their own advantage or profit. This can include—but is not limited to—movies, TV, book clubs, condensations, magazines, foreign translation, and so forth.

Syntax: The way in which words or phrases are put together. For example, it is considered incorrect to end a sentence with a preposition or prepositional phrase. I believe it was Winston Churchill who, irked at the absurdity of this rule, declared: "I will no longer up with it put."

Termination: (See Reversion of rights.)

Territory: A contractual definition specifying where the publisher has the right to sell your book in the English language.

Text: The work as a whole, minus front or back matter.

Third-person narrative: A book written from the viewpoint of "she" or "he."

Typeface: (Also known as font.) The size and appearance of a given kind of type; there are dozens to choose from, distinctive from one another in varying degrees. Each comes in several sizes, from the kind that your arms aren't long enough to read, to headline size.

Typeset: For centuries, this process was done by hand. A person hand-selected the letters necessary to complete a line of text, and added leading before commencing to set the next line. It became automated in this century, and of late, is giving way to computerized systems. One "sets your manuscript into type," but "the manuscript has been typeset."

Uppercase: Capitalized; either a letter or an entire word.

Unsolicited manuscript: Succinctly, it's "Who asked you!"

Widow: Infrequently found nowadays, but it is the top line of a page that has so few words that it doesn't even go halfway across. To the eye, it appears all alone and abandoned—a widow.

Word count: An estimate of how many words are contained in a manuscript; or a projection of how many words are to be typeset.

Wraparound cover: (See Cover artwork.)